"Therefore go and make disciples of all nations…"
- Jesus

THE TRUTH IS...

OTHER BOOKS BY STEVE

Marked: Discovering What It Means To Follow Jesus

Reasons For Christian Hope

Certain: Erasing Doubts of the Christian Faith

THE TRUTH IS...

SHARING THE TRUTH OF JESUS WITH CONFIDENCE, CONVICTION, AND COMPASSION

STEVEN KOZAK

ISBN: 978-1982072810

For more information about Steven Kozak or his ministries visit
www.stevenkozak.com

Cover Design: RocketPark Media

To my amazing family.
Countless night at the kitchen counter writing in between dinners,
parenting, and pauses in conversation. Thank you for your support,
love, and most of all, patience.

.

CONTENTS

PREFACE

I grew up in a Christian home. But I didn't stay there. By the time I entered high school, I began to walk away from the church. Simultaneously, as doubts began to enter my mind, as negative influences from friends and culture made a significant imprint, church became less of a priority and discipleship left by the wayside.

It wasn't until much later in life did I decide to investigate what the church claimed was true and where I found a true sense of belonging and community. My endless searching led me to seminary, apologetics, and eventually in ministry. It didn't take long for me to see the same doubts, questions, and search for truth in my students. Spending the last fifteen years in youth ministry, I can tell you from first-hand experience in nearly every arena of youth culture, there is a great need for worldview and apologetics training. Today's Christian students are faced with more significant challenges, higher amounts of stress, and even greater threats to their faith than ever before. Not only do students continue to ask profound and insightful questions, but they are also asking at an increasingly younger age. Questions once asked in college, or high school are now the questions of middle school students and sometimes younger.

However the challenge is not only convincing our students they need the skills and confidence to engage their culture with the gospel but our youth leaders as well. Parents, pastors, and teachers have to be prepared to answer and equip our young people. As leaders, we need to not be afraid to ask the hard questions and be prepared with a strong biblical worldview to address the significant issues of our time and our culture. Truth—which seems like it ought to be a clear black and white issue, is vastly grayer for our students. There is tremendous confusion surrounding identity, morality, and even the role of religion.

This is the whole reason I decided to write this book: prepare leaders to help students answer questions and further their walk with Christ. I don't want students to go through what I did. I came back to Christ, but most don't.

Over and over, I am asked for useful resources from parents and pastors who have tremendous desire but very little time. My hope is that this book provides you the necessary tools and knowledge without overwhelming you and consuming precious time. My goal was to combine content and method in an approachable format that can be talked about at the dinner table, small group, or classroom. There is a lifetime of resources available to anyone willing to take the time and energy to study. But there just isn't enough time to tackle it all. This will provide you with an excellent starting point.

More than ever we need youth who are well trained in what they believe and why and prepared to give an answer in their fast-paced, highly digitized culture. But equally, we need leaders who are prepared to train those students.

I provided you with conversation starters and ways to discuss and ideas to integrate apologetics into your ministry or family. Use them. Have your leaders read this. Give it to parents and teachers. The future may belong to the students, but it is our job to hand it off well.

INTRODUCTION
IT'S GRADUATION DAY

Her name was Jennifer. She was the star of the youth group. She was the leader, the role model; the one that both parents and pastor were convinced would be a much-needed light into the dark corners of university life. Naturally, Jennifer was commissioned and sent to the local public university. Everyone was confident that she would no doubt make a difference.

A semester later, the phone call came. "Dad, I am not sure I believe in Jesus anymore." Without panicking, Jennifer's dad questioned and probed—searching for the right thing to say to set his perfect daughter back on track. Her biggest reason for turning away from the church and the faith she had known her entire life was courtesy of one professor. She told her dad, "I had a smart professor that said we shouldn't believe in fairy tales if we are going to make it in the world of academia." That was all it took—one professor and one semester to erase eighteen years of Sunday school, youth group, and prayer.

What was missing? Neither Jennifer, her parents, or pastor saw what was coming. While so many of us wait for a problem to occur, then search for the antibiotic, the solution is in the inoculation—a proactive solution before there ever is a problem. The entire Christian community must work together to prepare our students for what they are guaranteed to experience after high school (or even in high school).

THIS ISN'T YOUR MOMMA'S YOUTH GROUP

This story and many others like have far too often come tragically true. For nearly a decade I had the privilege of shaking hands and giving hugs to every senior as they received their diploma and made their way across the graduation stage. Part of my job was to read a selected verse or passage the student chose after their name was read. I considered it an honor and privilege, but also a burden. I wondered how many of these students that I had to come to know so well and care about so much would turn out like Jennifer.

But why so much angst? After all, you and I can only have so much control and influence. These students have to make the Christian faith their faith, and that is not always a smooth ride into the sunset of eternal bliss. The path is narrow and the ride often bumpy. We worry because we believe that as teachers, pastors, parents, and mentors of students we are increasingly ill-equipped to successfully navigate our rapidly changing culture. In other words, this isn't your momma's youth group anymore. This isn't the youth group of the seventies, or the nineties, or even the youth group of the millennials.

The youth group that successfully attracted students through unique messaging, entertainment, games, super trendy and inviting spaces and relevant motivational talks by hipster youth pastors no longer have the same lasting impact. The worry that students are leaving the church in droves is no longer true—because they already left. The days of evangelical Christianity as the predominant religious affiliation are long over. That crown now belongs to those who wish to remove all identification—the *nones*. Millennials became famous by seeking a more authentic experience in church, community, justice, and a place of social equality. So we modeled youth group to fit those needs. Today, Generation Z, although they maintain some similarities to that of their elder generations are searching for identity and belonging. They are unsure of what truth is or where to find it and have been convinced that acceptance means affirmation—even if affirmation means immorality.

AS SIMPLE AS MAKING DISCIPLES

The job description of anyone who leads or mentors youth is simple. Make disciples—disciples who go and make disciples. I think that when you boil it down, we are not in the business of running great programs, writing books, crafting the most impactful retreats, or even publishing the most comprehensive curriculum. These are all just tools to help us in our mission to make disciples. However, these tools are only a part of what is needed.

Another critical element of that disciple-making process is preparing students to engage their world with the gospel, rather than conform to it, hide from it or run from it, by helping students look out into the world and see it through the eyes of Jesus. Disciple-making is about teaching students to understand what a Christian worldview looks like. When confronted with things like trust, truth, social issues, history, politics, family life, media, and morality; how can we walk with students so that they are being guided through life grounded in the reality of biblical truth?

Whether we choose to accept it or not, the world we knew as students is far different than the world our students are faced with today—with an entirely different set of presuppositions, a different set of moral standards, different ideas of truth, a different view of authority, and a different idea of the role the Bible plays in life. The list goes on. As a result, many of us have found ourselves staring at a generation we don't understand with challenges we have never faced or anticipated. We stand paralyzed in fear of the terrain before us. Maybe it wasn't what we expected. Maybe the theories taught in seminary are no longer relevant. Rest assured, regardless of the reason, you find yourself in good company. You are not alone.

Remember what the disciples were doing after Jesus had resurrected? John's gospel describes the disciples meeting in an upper room with the doors locked because they were afraid of the Jewish religious leadership— for a good reason. What would happen next? People recognized Peter. Maybe their crucifixion was next. The disciples were facing at unchartered terrain. Paralyzed in fear, they just waited. But then Jesus shows up and lays on them the missional responsibility to carry the work he started to the rest of the world (John 20:19). They had to change their entire ministry model. Everything they had learned to do with Jesus, they now had to do without him. The model may have changed, but the mission had not. It was still about going into the world and proclaiming the gospel. Jesus made disciples. It was now their turn to go and make disciples. We bear that same responsibility as we make disciples of our students. We are sent so that our students might be sent. But that sending requires not only a keen and thorough understanding of the Bible and what it means to live a morally upright life. It also means having the ability to understand and engage the world they live in every day without falling victim to it.

WHAT ARE WE UP AGAINST?

The disciples were up against the Jewish elite, the pagan religious practices of the Gentile world, and the Roman Empire. They had to figure out how a Jesus view of the world could infiltrate and transform that world. Our students' task is quite similar. They are up against secularism, skepticism, and alternative forms of spirituality. If my time spent with students over the years has taught me anything, it's that, despite how much students talk of their love for Jesus, a biblical worldview in areas like social sciences, psychology, politics, or history is highly questionable if not absent entirely.

Instead of a biblical worldview, students have been taught to create two spheres or compartments of life. One compartment is designed for our religious life. In it, we keep things like church, retreats, devotional time, prayer, and even those designated as church friends. This is our private life. It's the space we reserve for Jesus. The other compartment is where we keep the rest of our life. The public side of life—the life we share with the rest of the world.

Whether we have realized it or not, we have drawn a clear line in the sand between the secular and the sacred—and we have taught our students the same practice. Students, therefore, have no context for how to infiltrate and transform their world with the gospel. Houston Baptist professor and author, Nancy Pearcey describes students' weakness this way,

"The reality is that most students lack the sense of how Christianity functions as a unified, overarching system of truth that applies to every area of life. Instead, they hold to Christianity as a collection of truths, but not as Truth."[1]

But wait a minute. We have a youth group, Bible memory, retreats, games, cool youth spaces, small groups, and conferences. Isn't that enough? What about all the effort and investment churches are making into youth? Track with me for a moment and let's get further beyond the great programs and millions of dollars invested. Clearly, participation in church and technical proficiency of the Bible is a huge piece. But it is a piece. Imagine a beautiful classic Corvette or Mustang, without an engine. It is great to look at, has a ton of potential, but it sill needs an engine. Some people may never even notice and only admire the exterior, but that doesn't change the fact the car needs an engine. Teaching your students how to live and breathe a biblical worldview is the engine. It is the stuff under the hood, the stuff that most don't see or ever admire, yet is essential to go anywhere. In short, our students need to be taught to think like a follower of Jesus. They are wonderful worshippers, great prayers, selfless servants, but far too often give way to secularism when it comes to matters outside of the church building.

So what can we do? What can be done as pastors, youth leaders, and parents to be certain that when our students hit the pavement of the college campus, the corporate office or even the family gathering; they have the tools necessary to treat their everyday lives as a mission, and as a means to take the name of Jesus to the nations? How do you build an engine?

Through various books, my experience of trial and error and even suggestions from students themselves, I have tried at least a dozen different strategies and programs. All of which I had hoped would launch my ministry into an entirely new dimension of effectiveness. But of all of those ways—some worked, most failed—I have found two simple, yet very intentional pieces that year after year made the greatest, lasting impact. In other words, although some engines are bigger and more powerful than others, these key parts are essential for all of them.

First key. As leaders, we must explore with our students what a sanctified life means in their context. Not just in preparation for the life to come, but holiness for this life now. Following Jesus is not about tapping into a magic formula to catch your reserved flight to heaven. It is about a missional lifestyle that captures every part of life—every thought and action—and makes it obedient to Christ. Every step, in every sphere, walking as Jesus did. But a missional life cannot be taught; it must be caught. Students need to see you setting the example. They need to see you get it right. They even need to see you get it wrong from time to time. Remember what Paul said. "Follow my example, as I follow Christ's example" (1 Corinthians 11:1).

When I first started teaching, I was told that students don't care how much you know until they know how much you care. Today, I think that is only partially true. The millennial and digital generations are less impressed with the know-it-all on stage telling them how they should live and much less likely to seek out wisdom from on high. Instead, they want to see us humbly walk with them and participate. They are looking to be shown rather than told. They care about well we walk with them.

Second key. What if youth group was more of a training ground, or like an inoculation? Think about what your ministry could look like if you intentionally created "battle like" conditions in a controlled environment allowing students to wrestle with ideas, issues at school or home, even politics? Creating a training ground means helping students properly filter these things through a biblical worldview. Correct, rebuke, and train. Their missional success in this world begins with their preparedness now. Believe me. Students are eager to learn. In fact, their brains are hardwired for learning at a greater capacity now than at any point in their lives. They have questions and want answers. Challenge them. They will rise to it.

This is more than just a shift in thinking. It is a shift in lifestyle. We, as youth leaders, need to live missional and invite students into that space. Invite them into the challenges, the successes, and the failures. Invite them to follow your example as you seek to follow Christ. And then provide them opportunities to lead others. Show them what it means to see the world as Jesus does so they don't merely strive to just successfully survive the world, but transform it and redeem it for the kingdom of God.

There is no overnight solution, quick fix, or the new program to run that will fix everything and have students lined up as if the latest pop star was in town. Discipleship is a process. It is a process requiring relationships and a process that requires patience and careful planning. Confidence in your students venturing off to college and beyond takes rigorous and intentional training. That training starts here, and it starts now.

This book is designed as your starting point.

GETTING STARTED

First, let's be clear about what this book is not. I never intended this book to cover every square inch of material when it comes to training students to understand what they believe and why. Nor does this book answer every possible question. Instead, my desire in this book is to get the ball rolling. It is a starting point. Training our students in the world of apologetics and the art of sharing one's faith is neither a sprint nor a marathon. It is like 400-meter hurdle—how you start is vital to finishing well. Too slow, you'll never catch up, too fast and you'll run out of gas.

Assume for a minute that God does not exist, and Jesus was not real. Imagine that the world you occupy and enjoy was nothing more than a happy accident and religion nothing more than blind comfort for the weak minded. Salvation in Jesus aides in that crutch by deifying a mythological story of a man who may have claimed to be divine and whose followers devised a plan to falsely claim he came back from the dead. Maybe even go so far as to imagine that any definitive truth cannot exist, morals are a human construct, and the solution of evil rests in the evolution of the human brain to a higher state of existence and understanding. This is where I want to begin our journey together. Now I, of course, understand that if you have been a follower of Christ for any length of time, it is impossible to set aside your foundational principles by which you live and pretend they no longer exist. But I want you to at least get a glimpse of where I began this journey—from the beginning.

Together we are going to make the case that Christianity as a worldview provides the best possible answers to life's greatest questions. We will walk together exploring truth, doubt, the existence of

God, the nature of and reliability for the Bible, the problem of evil and suffering in the world, and the resurrection. Each chapter offers a comprehensive yet concise and easy to grasp treatment of the nature of the Christian worldview. However, we cannot limit learning to theory and general principles. My goal for this book is that you would use it, write in it, refer back to it, and as a result, grow in knowledge and practice.

To aid in this process, I have added a section at the end of each chapter designed to help guide conversations with your students. Whether you are a pastor, parent, small group leader, or teacher, the conversation starters are intentionally crafted to create dialogue. Additionally—and admittedly unorthodox—I provided you with some white space for notes, ideas, questions, objections, and reminders for further exploration. The best learning happens when we engage the material on several different levels. Reading this book will not be enough. Use it.

We all wonder if our students will graduate and turn out like Jennifer. My hope and prayer for this book is that you will no longer need to wonder. My prayer is that your students would strut across that stage not only confident to take on the world for the kingdom but eager.

CHAPTER ONE
PREPARED FOR A DEFENSE

DEFINING APOLOGETICS

Several years ago, I was helping my church's college ministry teach a class on evangelism. The curriculum was a basic run through about how to strike up the conversation and how to close it with an invitation to accept Jesus, using the typical Romans Road method.[2] After the class, one of the students approached me to clue me in on "how evangelism is done." His tactic was simple. He arrived at the local grocery store and mingled around the produce. He would wait until enough people gathered around one of the fruit or vegetable sections. At just the right moment he would blurt out, "Wow! Look at all the amazing fruit God has given us!" He hoped that his boldness would offer the opportunity to engage in a conversation with someone. If you're like me, the more curious nature of this episode is not if people got involved in the conversation, but how many people thought he was either joking or slightly insane.

I agree this action is incredibly bold, and I commend him for the effort, but the truth is that this method is not likely to produce fruit (pun intended). On the one hand, it is easy for us on the outside to critique his approach, but, on the other hand, very few of us would ever attempt it—not because we disagree with the method, but because we are fearful. Let's face it, sharing your faith, talking about Jesus or even mentioning God in a conversation is not easy, and at times, quite awkward.

Our minds and hearts are not prone to think about the things of God. They do not naturally think God's thoughts and our words and actions are not naturally in line with those of Jesus. Therefore, God and the reasons why we believe are not always a part of our natural train of thought, making for these awkward moments that so many of us dread and therefore, avoid. This is why Paul tells us to be transformed by the renewing of our minds (Romans 12:2). While the Spirit is an active agent in our lives, as we become complete in the image of God, God's plan is that we work in harmony and rhythm with the Spirit. He has chosen to use us in His plan to redeem all of creation. We are called to make disciples; we are called to give a defense, we are called to speak up; we are called to engage those who don't believe. This is apologetics.

For those who have heard of or practiced apologetics in any way, shape or form has no doubt read 1 Peter 3:15. This verse stands as the cornerstone for what Christians know to be the practice of apologetics.

"But in your hearts revere Christ as Lord. Always be prepared to give an answer to everyone who asks you to give the reason for the hope that you have. But do this with gentleness and respect, keeping a clear conscience, so that those who speak maliciously against your good behavior in Christ may be ashamed of their slander." - 1 Peter 3:15-16

Peter's first letter is directed at Christians who were persecuted in the first-century and had suffered for what they believed. Their faith rested in knowing that God had fulfilled His covenant promises to Abraham through Jesus and the consequent hope, that because of the resurrection of Jesus, death is not final. The persecution that first-century Christians endured proved not to be final. Because of Jesus' resurrection and God's covenant faithfulness, their hope rested in the future resurrection because Jesus defeated death. But in times of such suffering, just "declaring" Jesus would not be enough when asked of this hope.[3] It is here that Peter encourages his readers to give a full apologetic or defense for the certainty of their hope.

The key word in this verse for the apologist is "defense." In the Greek, it is ἀπολογίαν, pronounced "apologeean," from the Greek word apologia. This is where we get the term "apology." Commonly, we define apology as a written or spoken expression of one's regret, remorse, or sorrow for having insulted, failed, injured, or wronged another.[4] Typically when we think of an apology, we think of how we apologize to someone that we have wronged. However, when we are talking about Christian apologetics, we are not saying that "we're sorry" for what we believe, nor are we trying to argue someone into believing as we do.

I can imagine what many of you might be thinking, "Why would I need to defend my new found faith in Christ?" Besides, defending or arguing about the Christian faith seems to be a complete contradiction to Scripture. One should believe as a result of a transformed heart, not intellect. Right? Well, sort of.

An apology in ancient Greece was a legal defense against a formal charge. For example, the philosopher, Plato, recorded such a defense for Socrates in his *Apology*. "An apology involved formulating arguments and giving reasons in one's defense."[5] Essentially it was giving reasons for one's actions, thoughts and behaviors. So in the case of Christian apologetics, it involves providing a defense or reason for why we believe what we believe.

Even if we are not apologizing for being Christians, I imagine many of you might still be thinking, "I don't need to defend anything, I have faith!" Instead, maybe, you are comfortable with some uncertainty and fear because you are confident that God will give you the strength and words, so long as your willing to be used. Therefore, in your mind, there is no need for preparation, no need to purposefully engage non-believers, and no need to defend or convince people of your faith. After all, it is your faith, not theirs; the Spirit will work in their lives in God's time, and there is nothing you can do to alter that.

Despite these common questions and objections, the Apostle Peter told us always to be prepared to give an answer or defense to everyone who asks about the hope that you have (1 Peter 3:15). Jesus told us to go and make disciples of all nations (Matt 28:19, Acts 1:8). Seems simple, but there is something more significant underneath the surface of these commands—something that demands our attention and care. We should not presume that making disciples, building relationships, and even walking as Jesus did (1 John 2:6) is something that will just come naturally upon belief; or even something that magically happens through the Holy Spirit as if we are some puppet or robot controlled by God.

BIBLICAL SUPPORT FOR APOLOGETICS

Regardless of the seemingly countless objections to the study and practice of apologetics in the everyday Christian life, the concept, and discipline of apologetics is taken directly from the Scriptures and therefore is a vital part of the life of a disciple. If we study the model given to us in the Bible, we can see a defense of faith with Peter, Paul, and even Jesus. In large part, advocates of apologetics see 1 Peter as the only necessary proof that we as Christians need to "defend" our faith. Certainly, this should, and even could suffice. Peter reminded the early first-century Christians of the duty they had to be ready at any moment to defend the gospel—a fundamental and essential concept in a dangerous and volatile time for the church. But what about the ministry of the apostle Paul? Certainly, the great evangelist and author of the majority of the New Testament has something for us to learn from.

Paul's missionary efforts have provided the church with countless years of wisdom and examples for leadership, church planting, conflict resolution, practical living in light of the gospel, joy in suffering, and yes, even the practice of apologetics. For example, in Paul's first letter to the Corinthian church, he told them,

> "And so it was with me, brothers and sisters. When I came to you, I did not come with eloquence or human wisdom as I proclaimed to you the testimony about God. For I resolved to know nothing while I was with you except Jesus Christ and him crucified. I came to you in weakness with great fear and trembling. My message and my preaching were not with wise and persuasive words, but with a demonstration of the Spirit's power so that your faith might not rest on human wisdom, but on God's power." - 1 Corinthians 2:1-5

It almost seems abundantly clear that Paul is reminding a church that is divided, and focused on human accomplishment and status, that what matters is not our arguments, creative words, or knowledge; but, instead, with the power of the Spirit. At first glance, we might conclude that through Paul's example apologetics is not only unnecessary but unbiblical. Then it would seem that apologetics is undermining the work of the Holy Spirit. What might appear to be a problem passage regarding apologetics; what looks like Paul working to make a point that he did not try to persuade the people to believe in Jesus, but relied on the power of the Spirit; turns out to be only part of the story.

When we read Luke's account of Paul's visit to Corinth in Acts 18, we witness something entirely different. We get a much clearer picture of the story. In fact, we get the whole story.

> "After this, Paul left Athens and went to Corinth. There he met a Jew named Aquila, a native of Pontus, who had recently come from Italy with his wife Priscilla because Claudius had ordered all Jews to leave Rome. Paul went to see them, and because he was a tentmaker as they were, he stayed and worked with them. Every Sabbath he reasoned in the synagogue, trying to persuade Jews and Greeks." - Acts 18:1-4

To make sense of this we need to pay close attention to the context of both Paul's interaction with the Corinthians and Luke's record in Acts. In 1 Corinthians, Paul was addressing an issue of a division to people who found worth and personal entertainment in knowledge. Paul was simply reminding the Corinthian people that he did not stoop to their level when he brought the gospel. Instead, Paul let the power of God, through his words and efforts, make the impact. It is in Paul's visit to Corinth that we can see one of the clearest examples of apologetics through the building of relationships and community.

Paul had a knack for understanding the culture and the people that he was called to minister to. Wherever he went, he found a way to connect people to the gospel and provide reasons for belief and trust in Jesus. In his letter to the Corinthian church, Paul describes the value in knowing and using culture to connect the gospel to a particular people (1 Corinthians 9:21-23). In similar fashion to the passages above, Paul spoke to the Athenians in Acts 17. He took their current pagan worldview, poked a few holes in it and opened up doors for them to hear and understand just who this "unknown" god was.

> "Paul then stood up in the meeting of the Areopagus and said: "People of Athens! I see that in every way you are very religious. For as I walked around and looked carefully at your objects of worship, I even found an altar with this in-scription: TO AN UNKNOWN GOD. So you are ignorant of the very thing you worship—and this is what I am going to proclaim to you." – Acts 17:22-23

Paul did not shy away, get offended, or ignore the questions presented by the Athenians. He used their questions, found some truth in what they were saying, and turned it around to reflect the gospel. Paul did not force the gospel down their throats or condemn those who did not listen, nor did he bang on doors or make cold calls hoping that if he asked enough people some might believe. He simply took the opportunity to present a more complete view than the view they presently held.

The goal for Paul and the other apostles was to spread the gospel, as Jesus commanded, by emulating his life on earth through the empowerment of the Holy Spirit. The apostles and early believers thought it necessary to follow in the footsteps of Jesus, doing the things he did, and in some cases, even greater things (John 14:11-13). From the actions of Jesus, the apostles had all the evidence they needed to carry out the mission. Therefore, we can gain a great deal of instruction on how we should follow in those same footsteps, which of course applies to the practice of apologetics.

Read through each of the passages below carefully—notice how each of these point to believers engaging in the practice of apologetics.

"Dear friends, although I was keen to write to you about the salvation we share, I felt compelled to write and urge you to contend for the faith that was once for all entrusted to God's holy people." - Jude 3

"He must hold firmly to the trustworthy message as it has been taught so that he can encourage others by sound doctrine and refute those who oppose it." - Titus 1:9

"As was his custom, Paul went into the synagogue, and on three Sabbath days, he reasoned with them from the Scriptures, explaining and proving that the Messiah had to suffer and rise from the dead. "This Jesus I am proclaiming to you is the Messiah," he said. Some of the Jews were persuaded and joined Paul and Silas, as did a large number of God-fearing Greeks and quite a few prominent women." - Acts 17:2-4

"It is right for me to feel this way about all of you, since I have you in my heart and, whether I am in chains or defending and confirming the gospel, all of you share in God's grace with me." - Philippians 1:7

"The latter do so out of love, knowing that I am put here for the defense of the gospel." - Philippians 1:16

"Paul entered the synagogue and spoke boldly there for three months, arguing persuasively about the kingdom of God." - Acts 19:8

Even though this is not nearly a comprehensive list, I think it would be safe to assume that if we are trying to build a case for apologetics, we can be satisfied with the practice of perhaps the greatest apologist and evangelist the world has ever known. But what about Jesus?

SO THAT WE WOULD "KNOW"

As Christians, above all else, we are called to follow Jesus. So in the case of apologetics, we need to be sure that what we do in practicing apologetics aligns itself with the very actions of Jesus. We call this the Philosophy of Demonstration, meaning: we follow what Jesus does. For example, take a look at Mark 2:1-12.

"A few days later, when Jesus again entered Capernaum, the people heard that he had come home. [2]They gathered in such large numbers that there was no room left, not even outside the door, and he preached the word to them. [3]Some men came, bringing to him a paralyzed man, carried by four of them. ⁴Since they could not get him to Jesus because of the crowd, they made an opening in the roof above Jesus by digging through it and then lowered the mat the man was lying on. ⁵When Jesus saw their faith, he said to the paralyzed man, "Son, your sins are forgiven." ⁶Now some teachers of the law were sitting there, thinking to themselves, ⁷"Why does this fellow talk like that? He's blaspheming! Who can forgive sins but God alone?" ⁸Immediately Jesus knew in his spirit that this was what they were thinking in their hearts, and he said to them, "Why are you thinking these things? ⁹Which is easier: to say to this paralyzed man, 'Your sins are forgiven,' or to say, 'Get up, take your mat and walk'? ¹⁰But I want you to know that the Son of Man has authority on earth to forgive sins." So he said to the man, ¹¹"I tell you, get up, take your mat and go home." ¹²He got up, took his mat and walked out in full view of them all. This amazed everyone and they praised God, saying, "We have never seen anything like this!"

If you read the passage carefully, you should notice something significant about what Jesus is doing. Jesus certainly did not dispute the thinking of the teachers of the law on the point that God alone could forgive sins. Instead, Jesus replied, "that you may know that the Son of Man has authority on earth to forgive sins," (v. 10).⁶ Jesus does not expect the onlookers just to understand something, or to take his words by faith. Jesus uses his actions as a way to provide his disciples, the surrounding people, and even the Pharisees with *reasons* so that they will *know* just who Jesus is claiming to be. So the man gets up and goes home—in front of the entire crowd, leaving little doubt to those in attendance that Jesus had authority from God and, by implication, that he was the divine Son of God.

Jesus provided similar reasons to believe through various methods including miracles, prophecy, his lifestyle and example, authoritative teaching and reasoned argumentation. Take a minute and try to imagine Jesus coming to earth, growing up, beginning a ministry, and telling people that he is the Messiah and Savior of the world—and doing nothing to show he has any authority for such a claim. This, of course, is ridiculous. Instead, Jesus provides the nation of Israel, and every other surrounding nation, a reason to take notice that the Kingdom of God has come here and now. Similarly, Matthew 22:37-39 points to believers engaging with God and others through every facet of life, including the mind.[7] Christianity is not just a heart thing or a feeling; reason, logic, and faith make up the mind of a believer.

Countless passages throughout the gospels could be used to illustrate this concept of the Philosophy of Demonstration, but I think the clearest example of Jesus demonstrating a reason to believe stands with Thomas. Even as Jesus stood among his disciples, Thomas could not bring himself to a place where he fully believed and trusted that before him stood the risen Lord. He did the unthinkable, the unimaginable. He doubted. That is until Jesus gave him a clear reason.

"Now Thomas (also known as Didymus), one of the Twelve, was not with the disciples when Jesus came. So the other disciples told him, "We have seen the Lord!" But he said to them, "Unless I see the nail marks in his hands and put my finger where the nails were, and put my hand into his side, I will not believe." A week later his disciples were in the house again, and Thomas was with them. Though the doors were locked, Jesus came and stood among them and said, "Peace be with you!" Then he said to Thomas, "Put your finger here; see my hands. Reach out your hand and put it into my side. Stop doubting and believe." Thomas said to him, "My Lord and my God!" -- John 20:24-28

We can also see it in the Old Testament. Throughout the Old Testament, God frequently provides his people and surrounding nations the necessary evidence of who He is. Two popular passages come to mind. Shortly after Moses' introduction to God, he is instructed to appear in front of Pharaoh and demand the release of the Hebrew people from slavery. What comes next, most are certainly familiar with—a series of ten plagues that eventually wears down Pharaoh's stubbornness and he grants Moses' request. If you have seen the old *Ten Commandments* film with Charlton Heston, or the Dream Works production of *The Prince of Egypt,* you are at least familiar with the story. However, maybe the lesser-known part of this narrative is why. Out of all the ways God could have had His people released from the bondage of Egypt, why ten plagues? Why go through all the trouble of sending Moses back and forth? Why not just annihilate the Egyptians with fire from heaven just like Sodom and Gomorrah?

The reason for such an odd series of events comes in Exodus 7:5. "Then the Egyptians will know that I am the Lord when I extend my hand over Egypt and bring the Israelites out from among them." The plagues were more than just the miraculous means of getting Israel out of sticky situation. Each of the plagues was a direct smack in the face of the Egyptian gods. Whatever means of worship Egypt had—the Nile, the sun, etc.—God sought to illustrate to Pharaoh and the rest of Egypt that He was greater than all of them. God's purpose is more than just the release of Israel; it is so that Egypt (and Israel) may know Yahweh. But keep in mind; God does not limit his demonstrations to first impressions.

In an epic showdown to determine who deserved the rightful name of God and prove to King Ahab and the rest of the kingdom that worshipping Baal is an empty and useless pursuit, the prophet Elijah challenges the prophets of Baal to a divine dual. Everyone agrees that the "god who answers by fire—he is God" (1 Kings 18:24). The stage is set, and the contestants are ready. Home court advantage goes to the prophets of Baal, and they get to go first. A bull is placed on the altar if fire comes down from heaven—game over. However, despite the grand efforts of these prophets, their god seems much too busy, unable, and even unwilling. Even after Elijah taunts the prophets and their god, there is still no response. Elijah then takes center stage. He prepares the altar for the main event. But before he calls on God, he ups the ante. He instructs his servants to dump several gallons of water on the prepared alter—just to be sure that there is no confusion when God flips the switch and burns up the sacrifice. Elijah has water dumped, not once. Not twice. But three times. Once the sacrifice is fully prepared, Elijah prays.

> "Lord, the God of Abraham, Isaac, and Israel, let it be known today that you are God in Israel and that I am your servant and have done all these things at your command. Answer me, Lord, answer me, so these people will know that you, Lord, are God and that you are turning their hearts back again." - 1 Kings 18:36-37

Elijah's goal here is two key things. First, he wants onlookers to know God, to be certain of who God is and what he is capable of. Secondly, this knowledge would draw the people (not just Israel) close to God and give their allegiance to Him, by giving their hearts back to Him. In other words, knowledge leads to repentance, and it is God who provides the people with the means of knowing for certain who He is. Both are clear examples of God providing clear and sufficient evidence that the God of Abraham, Isaac, and Jacob is the only God worthy of worship and praise.

CONCLUSION

If you are at all like me, you won't be scoping out your local grocery stores to set up shop as your new center for evangelism. Nor are you going to train students to do the same. Although I have great respect for my friend who raved about God's creation to anyone who would hear, the reality is that most of us find ourselves stuck between what we know we ought to do and what we are prepared to do. But standing by and doing nothing is not an option and simply bringing people to church is not enough. Diving into apologetics helps us get unstuck.

Regardless of how unprepared or ill-equipped, we feel, each of us has been called to the divine responsibility to disciple our students helping them to engage and change their world. Ignoring vital pieces of making disciples like apologetics will no doubt have dire consequences for our students and our ministries.

I am sure it would be a safe bet that at some point in your life you were faced with something new, something unknown, something uncertain. But, the more reasons you had for not being afraid the more apt you became to try that something new. Apologetics is very much the same. As you begin to study the practice and discipline of apologetics, you will have a sense of fear—fear of rejection, fear of failure, or even the fear of doubt. However, the greater your certainty of the Christian claims to truth are, the greater your impact on the lives of others will be. The greater your reasons for believing in Jesus and having faith in the promises of God, the greater you will communicate those truths to the people God places in your life. Apologetics is meant to remove fear and unleash the Spirit of God within you with a greater power and a greater love. Apologetics is a fundamental part of what it means to follow Jesus as a disciple and when we engage in it in the right way we enter into a wonderful partnership with God and His mission.

CONVERSATION STARTER

Every belief requires a reason. If you believe that your car will start every morning, you have a reason you believe that. Faith in Christ (or lack of) is the same thing. You ought to have a reason. It is a heavy question, but it is also the appropriate place to start. Ask your students to think about and discuss the following question:

Why do you believe what you believe?

CHAPTER TWO

DOUBT: NAVIGATING THE UNSEEN

SEEDS OF DOUBT

We all know the look. You're engaged in conversation, trying your best to talk about Jesus, but you get the look. The look is the equivalent of a non-verbal scream, "I doubt it!" The person you are talking to has nearly tuned out, waiting for you to take a breath so that they can tear your worldview apart. So they hope. After the look come the questions. Questions that carefully and strategically plant seeds of doubt in your mind. You begin to think, "Am I being arrogant and exclusive?" "Could there be more than one way to God?" Or, "Is it possible that Jesus didn't exist at all?" There could be countless questions thrown at you, each designed to make you think twice about your confidence in what is unseen.

A seed of doubt does not have to be the end of the world until it begins to be fed, and grow. You recognize the legitimacy of these question posed by your adversary, so you write them down, tuck them into your tattered Bible, and wait for Sunday morning. Surely a pastor or ministry leader would have the answer, and once again, confidence would be restored, and your adversary is branded ignorant and uninformed.

But, instead of sure-fire, credible, and in-depth answers to such potential faith destroying questions, you received another "look." But this time the look was one of disappointment and contempt. The body language this time around, sadly grumbles, "How could you, a good Christian, ask such questions? How could you doubt?" Your pastor gives you a courtesy smile of disappointment and offers you nothing more than Christian self-help guidance and a few resources. Instead of fact-based historical and theological truth, you were told to pray and "just trust God." Instead of answering your questions, the best advice you get is to stop letting Satan create doubt in your mind. Leaving you with more questions and even a sense of, "Am I doing this all wrong?"

Of course, this scenario is not the case for every student, in every youth group. Nor is it true of every youth pastor. There are, of course, many pastors, churches, and even parents that provide excellent resources and answers. For many who have questions within the church are all too often glazed over with superficial answers and judgmental eyes. Consequently, students are left with one of two thoughts. Either something is wrong with them, or something is wrong with Christianity. Far too often this is the narrative I hear from students over and over.

YOU OF LITTLE FAITH

Doubt is poison to one's faith. Or so Christians are led to believe. Some would argue that the greatest hindrance to a faith that can move mountains is doubt. Therefore, generally speaking, Christians are not supposed to doubt. In fact, it could be that it is so uncommon, that it takes pastors and youth leaders by surprise when a student raises questions of doubt. Students are called to walk on water, to cast out fear, to not be like Peter, who given a chance to do something great, something no one has ever done before, doubted, began to sink, and needed to be rescued. Therefore, some believe doubt to be a sign of weakness and being uneducated. After all, if Christianity is claiming to possess absolute truth, then what reason would anyone have to doubt truth? Doubt only distorts the truth. If this is the case, then the responsibility of the Christian is to speak the truth in love and resist the evil temptation to doubt.

When Peter made his debut attempt to walk on water and failed, Jesus' response was not, "nice try," but, "you of little faith, why did you doubt?" (Matthew14:31). This famous passage is commonly interpreted that a true believer and follower of Jesus would not, maybe even could not, doubt. Some even go so far as to pin doubt as the antithesis of faith. Interpreting Matthew 14 this way makes Peter out to be a faithless fool who should have been able to not only walk on water, but tap dance, and do a few backflips. This understanding is then coupled with the moment John the Baptist is faced with his death and wonders if he is giving up his life for truth or a lie.

> "John's disciples told him about all these things. Calling two of them, he sent them to the Lord to ask, "Are you the one who is to come, or should we expect someone else?" When the men came to Jesus, they said, "John the Baptist sent us to you to ask, 'Are you the one who is to come, or should we expect someone else?'" - Luke 7:18-20

It would seem that John, after spending his entire professional life preaching the coming of Jesus, now somehow doubts that Jesus is, in fact, the Messiah. This, of course, opens the door for others in both

Old and New Testaments as suspects of doubt. What do we say about Job, about Abraham's insistence to fulfill God's promise by his means, Gideon, the nation of Israel as they feared crossing the Jordan into the Promised Land? What do we say of the disciples who decidedly scattered from the scene of the crucifixion and locked themselves in a room in fear? What about Thomas, commonly named doubting Thomas? Looking at the Bible in such a light can only lead one to conclude that doubting is nothing short of a destructive device used to distract Christians from the mission of making disciples. However, nothing could be further from the truth.

GREAT DOUBTS CAN CREATE GREAT FAITH

Traditionally when we think of doubt, we think of its meaning as a lack of certainty or conviction of a person or belief. So, in our case, doubt would amount to a lack of certainty about Jesus, his resurrection, the authority of the Bible, etc. Generally when we comment, "I doubt it," we mean to express a negative. "I doubt that I can go tomorrow." Or, "I doubt I'll get an A in this class." However, to doubt can be slightly different. If we take the meaning of doubt literally, having doubt, raising doubt, or saying, "I have my doubts," it can also be simply expressing uncertainty without committing. Doubt is usually expressed when absolute certainty is absent. In other words, to doubt Christianity is to remain skeptical of its truth and therefore to remain neutral and noncommittal. But this is not to say that certainty or confidence cannot be achieved or found. Just that it is not currently present. Let's revisit Matthew 14

"Lord, if it's you," Peter replied, "tell me to come to you on the water."

"Come," he said. Then Peter got down out of the boat, walked on the water and came toward Jesus. But when he saw the wind, he was afraid and, beginning to sink, cried out, "Lord, save me!" Immediately Jesus reached out his hand and caught him. "You of little faith," he said, "why did you doubt?" – Matthew 14:28-31

First, let's cut Peter a little slack. He was walking on water. He was doing the impossible. The context of the passage suggests that in the moment, Peter lost his head a little and despite Jesus being directly in front of him, he momentarily wavered in his ability to trust Jesus, that through Jesus, he could, in fact, do the impossible. This moment, although one of significant doubt, does not somehow propel Peter into a downward spiral of doubts about his faith in Jesus as Messiah. Instead, it becomes a moment of teaching that serves as evidence for everyone else (including Peter) about who Jesus claims to be. After the incident is over and both Jesus and Peter are back in the boat, the disciples, in a bit of shock and awe about what just transpired, comment, "Truly you are the Son of God" (Matthew 14:33). Rather than a rebuke for doubting, it stands as a picture of the life of every disciple. There is a fine line between disciples' absolute obedience and the terror of doing what our limited minds conceive as impossible. Our doubts find their home on this fine line.

But what about John? For John, his doubts weren't surrounded by a moment of crazy obedience to do the impossible. Wasn't he certain that Jesus was the Messiah? The key here is to look at the response Jesus gives to John's disciples. He does not rebuke, express disappointment, or laugh in their faces. Jesus simply responded with evidence,

> "So he replied to the messengers, "Go back and report to John what you have seen and heard: The blind receive sight, the lame walk, those who have leprosy are cleansed, the deaf hear, the dead are raised, and the good news is proclaimed to the poor. Blessed is anyone who does not stumble on account of me." - Luke 7:22-23

Jesus rattles off several pieces of evidence that, in Jesus, the kingdom was coming indeed. He essentially gave John exactly what he needed to hear. He assured him of what he already knew or thought to be the case. John knew who Jesus was, but in his moment of facing death, he wanted to be sure. John identified his doubts and adequately dealt with them. So instead of John facing his death uncertain, Jesus gave him the opportunity to face his death with absolute certainty.

Those who assert that doubt can be dangerous are not necessarily wrong. Doubt can be hazardous. However, doubt can also create incredible advantages. Doubt not properly dealt with can, and often will, lure someone away from truth. This is precisely the example I gave at the beginning of the chapter. Students need answers because students (and everyone else) have doubts. It is how we deal with that doubt that is vital to being a follower of Jesus. I think it is somewhat comforting to see passage after passage in the Bible of people who expressed doubt. But for every expression of doubt, there is provided a means to deal with it.

HOW TO DOUBT

I follow Jesus, not because I think he is a great moral philosopher with some solid principles on how to live a quality life; but because I believe that his claim to be the way, the truth, and the life, are in fact true. It is one thing to contemplate the abstract questioning of God, his existence, salvation, etc.; but it is an entirely different thing to experience life in such a way significant doubts are raised that require an answer.

There are many, if not most, Christians who express some doubt surrounding their faith in the course of their lives. Some of that doubt is based on circumstances; others are based on lack of knowledge—yet all it can and should be confronted. Theologian and professor, Alister McGrath notes, "Doubt is probably a permanent feature of the Christian life. It's like a kind of spiritual growing pain. Sometimes it recedes into the background; at other times it comes to the forefront, making its presence felt with a vengeance."[8] So then, how should we properly deal with our doubts?

Ask the tough question. Doubts may make its presence felt with a vengeance, but there is no need to fear them or fear to ask tough questions as a result of them. If one person does not like the question, or cannot answer, find someone that will. Questions are part of the academic exercise of faith, which is all too often left behind for a brand of faith that is entirely fueled by emotionalism. Emotions that are not grounded in the intellect create a sort of schizophrenic faith. However, doubt is not the antithesis of faith, but rather, having doubts and asking tough questions about God is vital to Christian maturation.

Choose whom you are asking to answer your questions wisely. You have more information at your hands than any other period in history. You can ask anyone anything. It was only a few years ago that connecting to the World Wide Web took considerable effort and was restricted to the bulky desktop computer at home or school. Today internet access is about as common as indoor plumbing. We find it odd when we are not connected. The more connected we are, the more information we have available to us. The kid who once asked mom and dad every possible question is now first turning to Google, Siri, or Alexa for answers. Based on the sheer volume of information available, students have no problem finding any answer they want and squeezing it into whatever worldview they wish to have rather than the worldview that represents truth. Information provides us with incredible opportunity and resources, but can also be incredibly dangerous.

Be willing to accept the tough realities. Jesus never said the call of discipleship was going to be easy. It is a lot easier to gossip about people, speak evil of them, shame them, or blatantly ignore them. After all, it makes us feel better about ourselves. So it can be slightly annoying when I am reminded to love my neighbors and pray for my enemies. With so much information at our disposal, it is easy to simply dismiss answers we don't like or only hold ourselves responsible in ways that we choose. However, this does not always line up with reality. Two plus two is always four, whether you like it or not. Truth is true, whether you like it or not.

This makes truth sometimes difficult to swallow. As was often the case, all kinds of people sought out Jesus and expressed their desire to follow him—whether people thought he was the Messiah or not didn't always matter. Even the Pharisees knew there was just something different about him. But despite their intense desire, the reality of following Jesus was often too much for some to handle, including the rich young man in Mark chapter 10.

"As Jesus started on his way, a man ran up to him and fell on his knees before him. "Good teacher," he asked, "what must I do to inherit eternal life?" "Why do you call me good?" Jesus answered. "No one is good—except God alone. You know the commandments: 'You shall not murder, you shall not commit adultery, you shall not steal, you shall not give false testimony, you shall not defraud, honor your father and mother.'" "Teacher," he declared, "all these I have kept since I was a boy." Jesus looked at him and loved him. "One thing you lack," he said. "Go, sell everything you have and give to the poor, and you will have treasure in heaven. Then come, follow me." At this, the man's face fell. He went away sad because he had great wealth." - Mark 10:17-22

This man's status and wealth were not necessarily the problem. It was his unwillingness to let it go. He was certain that he had it all figured out, but when Jesus presented him with a challenge, it proved to be too much. The questions might be tough, the answers might be tougher.

Don't be discouraged if some questions have unclear or incomplete answers. Sometimes questions just simply cannot be answered. We might not know why God does something or allows something to happen to others or us. We might not be able to answer why some people respond to the gospel and others reject it. The Bible does not teach explicitly on every possible topic we might encounter now and in the future. It was not designed that way. For example, why doesn't Jesus provide more detail about heaven? I am sure he could have if he chose to. But I have little doubt that if he did, we would surely be more focused on getting to heaven rather than focused on

God's kingdom here on earth. Jesus purposed us with a mission, in his sovereignty; we must trust that he has provided us all the information we need to know.

Allow your intellect to run the show rather than your emotions. Emotions are important, and we should consider them a gift from God. But a consistent worldview is not made up of emotions. Otherwise, we might find ourselves changing worldviews with every changing emotion of the day or moment. A consistent and life guiding worldview is built on intellect. Doubts fueled by emotions cannot be properly channeled and answered.

CONCLUSION

Let's revisit the example at the beginning of the chapter. There is no question that there will be times when seeds of doubt enter our worldview. There will most certainly be times when the conversations we engage in will cause us to take a second glance at a particular doctrine, our answers to social issues, or even our complete system of beliefs. But what I think becomes very clear in Scripture is that questions can be asked and doubts can be handled. We need not fear them. If Christianity were not true, if Jesus was some mythical or legendary figure, then there would certainly be cause for alarm the minute a significant question is raised. However, if Christianity is true if Jesus truly is the way, the truth, and the life (John 14:6), then there is no question the Christian worldview cannot handle.

So then, have your doubts. Ask your questions. But find the right place and people, get your answers, be ready for the tough realities, and keep your emotions guided by your intellect. Not only will you successfully navigate doubt, but also your faith and trust in Christ would increase exponentially.

CONVERSATION STARTER

It is important to remember that we all have our doubts. However, it is more important that we learn to express those doubts. As one who leads and mentors students you have the responsibility to create a safe place for students to express those doubts without judgment or condemnation. And the best ways to make that happen is to express your doubt first.

In what ways have you struggled with your faith recently? What would your faith in Christ look like if you had all of your questions answered?

CHAPTER THREE

WORLDVIEWS: SEEING HOW OTHERS VIEW THE WORLD

I loved playing football in high school. I loved the Friday night lights, the cool air, and the crack of the pads. I love the struggle, the victories, and even the defeats. I loved the friendships created, the band of brothers that stuck through high school together. We had each other's back. I remember after Friday night home games, most of the team would meet at one of the local buffet restaurants in town. Where else would forty hungry high school football boys go to eat as much as possible for as little as possible?

There are two incredible things about a buffet restaurant; the unending selection of food and the unlimited number of plates you could fill. Any other restaurant you are handed a menu and forced to make a selection. Once it's made, you have to live with it. With the buffet, you can try as much as you like. You can eat as much or as little as you would like, try something new, or eat the same thing every time. The choice is yours. And that is the point—it is all about choice and a lack of commitment.

In over a decade of teaching, I soon realized that many of my students saw the world much like how I ate from a buffet. Without even realizing or fully understanding it, their view of the world was being formed by a constant stream of information, picking and choosing what sounds good or was appealing to the lifestyle they desired. This is true now more than it was ten years ago. This makes our efforts to communicate the gospel that much more difficult.

How much easier it would be to simply learn the most popular worldviews or religions and how to best communicate the gospel to those groups. However, in a world that is more diverse than ever, the dividing lines between differing worldviews and religions are much less clear. So exclusively learning about overarching belief systems should give way to building positive relationships with individuals. In other words, allow what a person thinks and how they live to inform you of their worldview and how best to communicate the gospel, rather than letting a worldview or religious ideology inform you what you think about them and how to share the gospel.

THE VALUE OF RELATIONSHIPS

The art of apologetics is not about pushing your agenda. Apologetics, instead, is about a reasoned defense of Christianity in the context of personal dialogue and relationships.[9] It is virtually impossible to talk about Jesus to a professed atheist without any prior knowledge of him. Equally, there is no need to try to prove that God exists to a Muslim. In our Western obsession with spirituality, you will no doubt find several people who will profess to believe in God and even *know* God. Only to find out later that they are talking about a god, and you are talking about the God of Scripture and the incarnate God, Jesus Christ. Taking a pragmatic, results-oriented approach will likely not reveal any of those incredibly important details of that person.

But what if you took the time to get to know people? What if you took the time to ask questions about why they believe what they believe? What if you stopped shoving Jesus down their throat, maybe even dare not mention Jesus until the time was just right? More than just forming friendships to have a chance to introduce the gospel, this relational approach to apologetics will help you guide the conversation, build trust, and craft your apologetic arguments to suit that person's needs.

Of course, to do this, you need a knowledge base. Preparedness requires knowledge and making disciples requires a relationship. The combination of these two takes apologetics from theory to practice. Therefore, we begin with creating a knowledge base. Not only a knowledge of what you believe and why, but what others believe. Making disciples, sharing the gospel, or doing the work of a Christian apologist requires helping others make sense out of the data of the reality of life. In other words, to explain the world—or help someone else explain it—you first need to understand how reality is interpreted. Our view of reality informs us of how we deal with life's "stuff," big and small. How to communicate, how to deal with stress, raise a family, function at school, deal with life and death, maturing, differentiating between what is right and wrong, etc.; all begin with how we see the world. It begins with our worldview.

WHAT IS A WORLDVIEW?

One of my favorite movie franchises is the *Rocky* movies. I have been watching these since I was a kid. I am a sucker for underdog movies and the inspirational motivation it provides. But as I have grown older, I have come to appreciate the movies at a much deeper level.

Throughout the entire franchise, there is one overarching story at play. In the sixth movie installment, Rocky is talking to his son. Rocky's life has taken a different turn, he is back in Philadelphia, no longer married, no longer rich, and is not all that close to his son. But in this one moment, Rocky articulates sort of the ongoing theme of each of these movies. In a moment of trying to help his son navigate some difficult waters, he reminds him, "It's not how hard you can hit, but hard you can get hit and keep moving forward...that's how winning is done."[10] This single statement encompasses Rocky's entire worldview. A worldview that is played out in each of the movies, where all too often he took hit after hit in the ring and kept fighting until his opponent was worn out. This relentless determination to never give up is the lens through which Rocky views reality. It is how he sees the world.

The same could be said of the now famous *Marvel Cinematic Universe*. In the film, *Captain America: Civil War*, we witness, first hand, a clash of worldviews among friends. Or in Marvels, *Spider-Man* comics, Peter Parker is continuously reminded of his uncle Ben's famous phrase, "with great power comes great responsibility."[11] This, again, is a worldview statement. Peter is often confronted and conflicted between what he wants and what he sees as his responsibility.

Each of these examples gives some dressing to Norm Geisler's basic but effective definition of a worldview. "How one views or interprets reality."[12] The word, worldview comes from the idea of a paradigm of life, or the pair of glasses we use to see and interpret everything. It is one's view of the world, one's view of reality, how they see things and how they interact with the world. A worldview answers the big questions of life. Even if, like most people, you're not thinking of questions like, "Who am I," or "What is the meaning of life," a coherent and plausible worldview will seek to answer these kinds of questions even if the answer is on a subconscious level. James Sire, in his book *The Universe Next Door*, describes a worldview as,

> "...a commitment, a fundamental orientation of the heart, that can be expressed as a story or in a set of presuppositions which we hold about the basic constitution of reality, and that provides the foundation on which we live and move and have our being."[13]

Although this definition is loaded with meaning and could require several pages to unpack, it essentially is the backdrop of the story or narrative that guides life.[14] However, this story must explain reality; remain logical and coherent in that explanation, offer facts to back these assertions and, at the same time refrain from contradiction. Of course it is in theory that a worldview flows perfectly and plausibly, but in reality, people's views of the world can often be as varied as the local buffet restaurant, confused, and as clear as mud.

Just like the buffet line, everyone eats something; everyone has a worldview. This is not a question of religion—as even the most irreligious people still possess a worldview. Anytime, anywhere we attempt to answer a question—as simple as "where's my wallet," to as complex as, "who am I,"—is operating from a worldview framework. It is the means by which we begin to understand ourselves and how we come to have knowledge about the world around us. Therefore, worldviews must be comprehensive in every detail, large or small. Abu Murray, in his book *Grand Central Question*, comments,

"Worldviews must be comprehensive. It has to address all facets of life's main questions, from the broad ideas to the minute details. If a belief system fails to address all the central questions of life, it fails to be a view of the world, because it leaves significant aspects of existence unaddressed."[15]

In other words, any belief system that fails to address the central questions of life fails to be a valid and plausible worldview.

Our view of the world and the guiding of our understanding of the way things are cannot contradict itself in one or more of its answers to the fundamental questions of life. In other words, answers to one kind of question should not contradict with our answers to another kind of question. For example, how we view human life cannot contradict with humanity's purpose in life. If a person has any contradiction, it should serve as a red flag for that person's views in one or more areas of life. In this case, a person's belief is no longer justified. Ironically many people fail to stick to one particular worldview, jumping from one ideology to the next, based on emotion, rather than a logical framework.

WHY SHOULD I LEARN DIFFERENT WORLDVIEWS?

There was a time when one's worldview was passed on from parents and the surrounding community (churches, schools, etc.). How one saw the world was solidified long before they ventured out into the world. In our twenty-first-century world, this is no longer true. Instead, our world has unprecedented opportunities to question and to find faults or doubts in what we learned at home and school. The more information available to us, and the high rate it reaches us provides a much wider variety of information in which to answer life's most important questions. Our culture is no longer forced to work through the questions and issues of life given a particular worldview embedded in us at a very young age. Instead, we can ride the emotional tide and search endlessly until we discover what it is that our itching ears want to hear. Now imagine what that does for our students who are native users of a high tech, instant information world.

We are left with potentially countless variations within most of the major worldviews. From Christian to Muslim to Atheist, no one person's view is entirely consistent with another. A person may call himself a Hindu. However, a comparison of his thoughts to mainstream Hinduism may result in a realization that this person is actually farther from mainstream Hindu beliefs and integrates views from other surrounding worldviews from his culture. So, if all you know is mainstream Hinduism and you approach an alleged Hindu in such a manner, you may miss an opportunity to connect with him on a deeper level, and therefore, miss an opportunity to share the gospel.

So instead of learning worldviews as some predetermined ideological paradigms, spend time asking questions. The more questions you ask, the more information you will find. The more information you find, the greater chance you have at finding the flaws in their worldview. The more flaws you find, the greater chance you will have for offering the Christian worldview and the gospel message. With the right tactics and enough practice, you will even find that many people actually discover for themselves that their way of thinking is incorrect in some fashion or has areas of truth that line up with the Christian view.

This approach also prevents us from judging others or making snap decisions about who someone is or what they believe. The gospel is best communicated when we develop the context of relationships. The more we know about someone, the better chance we have of communicating the truth of Jesus to him. Our goal is to come alongside and truly know who a person is, instead of classifying them and shoving Jesus down their throat, seeking to make a convert instead of a disciple. Within relationships come incredible opportunities for the gospel to come naturally and authentically.

RELIGION OR WORLDVIEW

What about religions? Isn't a worldview just an academic way of talking about different religions? After all, some worldview systems are in fact considered a religion as well. This is the case with Christianity. There is a specific Christian worldview as well as what some may call the Christian religion. However, atheism is also a worldview, but most do not consider it a religion. The Oxford dictionary defines religion as a belief in and worship of a superhuman controlling power, especially a personal God or gods.[16] Additionally, religion is often thought of humanity's dependence on God, or at a minimum, the desire for that dependence through rituals, ceremonies, and doctrine. Fundamentally, religion assumes the existence of some higher power that is sought out to fulfill the desires of the people.

So, how does a worldview differ from a religion? Our worldview informs our religious views. It takes us from conception to practice. Therefore, for some people, their religion is the outworking of their worldview. For others, their lack of religion is the product of their worldview. Therefore, not only do we need to understand the nature of several of the world's major religions, but we also need to understand where they fit into the catalog of worldviews. This helps us to develop authentic relationships with non-Christians and helps us to communicate the gospel more effectively.

SOME OF THE MOST COMMON WORLDVIEWS

Since so few people have clear-cut and well-thought-out worldviews, a key principle in apologetics is to gather as much information as possible from the person you are talking to in a very short amount of time. Even some Christians, have the "buffet worldview," themselves taking a little from wherever they like: what they read, who they associate with, and how their experiences have shaped them. However, before we begin to ask questions to determine their worldview, we must have a basic understanding of the most popular views. These views will provide for us a basic framework as we engage people in conversations regarding their worldview.

Theism: God created the universe and everything in it. This is the starting point for a Christian worldview—a person who believes in God. But, keep in mind, just because a person says they believe in God, does not necessarily mean they are a disciple of Jesus Christ. Professing belief and living in light of that belief are very different things.

Finite Godism: Much like the theist, Finite Godism believes that God created the universe and is active in it. However, that activity and creative abilities are limited in scope and power. They deny the miraculous and cite evil as the reason for believing in God's limited power—God is finite. And because God is thought to be finite, he is much more of an image of man's concept and a means of marrying the idea of the divine with relative morality.

Pantheist: God is the world, meaning he is in everything and therefore, is literally the universe. Think of it as if god is every tree, rock, soda can, animal, and even people. Often this is where New Age philosophy is born—the idea that we can become a god.

Atheist: God does not exist. The true atheist is absolutely sure of that fact. You will find that though many people will say they are atheists, they really are not. Those who claim to be atheists because they hate are mad at, or simply reject God, are not necessarily atheists. The essential principle of atheism is to not recognize in any way, shape or form any god, of any kind. Atheist includes naturalism and secular humanism.

Agnostic: God might exist. The agnostic view can be summed up in the statement, "I don't know if there is a God." There are actually two kinds of agnostics, soft and hard. A soft agnostic asserts that they just *do not know* if there is a God. This view can be beneficial because it usually means they are open to arguments, proofs or possibilities of other worldviews. On the other hand, a hard agnostic claims one *cannot* know whether God exists. The latter is stubborn, and the former is not.

Deist: God created the universe, but is not personal. Like a watchmaker, he made the watch, set things in motion and left. This view has various philosophies but essentially surrounds the idea that God was, in fact, the first cause of the universe but has no dealings with his creation whatsoever.

Postmodern: This perspective is doubtful and skeptical of any grounded theoretical perspectives or worldviews.[17] If the modern era was certain through art, science, literature, and philosophy, then the postmodern rejects all such claims to certainty.

So, where does one's particular religion fit into these categories? For the most part, each religion will fit into one (or more) of the categories listed above. For example, Hindu's are considered pantheists, while Jews and Muslims are considered theists. I would argue that most people do not stick to one solid worldview and instead indulge in the buffet—an all you can eat menagerie of theories and ideologies. Although, academically, we would require people's worldviews to be consistent; that is rarely the case—even among Christians.

WORLDVIEW QUESTIONS

So far we have discovered that many people's worldviews are a mixed bag. We have also discovered that an individual's worldview is best discovered in the context of relationship. But how do engage in a conversation that is not only focused on worldview discovery but also relationally driven? Before we can defend anything, or make a case for our worldview, we need to have an understanding of what others think and why. Since people are not usually defined by one specific worldview, we need to ask a series of questions to help us, as well as them, to determine what their answers are to some of the most important questions in life, like why we are here and what happens at death. Listed below are five specific questions designed to unveil a person's worldview that reveal hints of different philosophies and religions, and you may even discover how they came to adopt those ideas.

Asking these questions provides us an excellent foundation from which we can begin to understand how another sees the world and how it is different or similar to our view.[18]

How would you describe the world around us? This question frames up the majority of a person's worldview. Although this question can be confusing for some, answers will describe the way in which a person sees the overall world.

Where did the world come from, and how would you describe people? This question speaks directly to whether the person believes in the existence of God, without explicitly asking the question.

How do you view the possibility of life after this one? This question gets to the heart of the matter for many. Issues like heaven and hell are likely to arise, as well as ideas of reincarnation and even the dismal reality of the atheistic belief that there is nothing after death.

How do we "know" anything, like right and wrong? Often a topic avoided, but incredibly important as this issue of knowing things like morality leads directly to one's view of God. This can open doors for the gospel.

Where is humanity headed? Is there hope for the planet? Are things better or worse? Answers can range all over and help us determine a person's overall view of the purpose of humanity on earth.

There are several versions of these questions, but all with the same goal in mind—worldview discovery and finding entry points for the gospel. The order of questions, the wording, and the way you approach them should fit the situation. I have had former students that memorized each question in their listed order and asked each accordingly. I have had others that focus on the intent of each question and only those that seem relevant for that moment. The point here is not a plug-and-play, prescribed system. Inserting that kind of method would compromise making an authentic, personal connection with the person you are speaking with.

CONCLUSION

Worldviews have a tremendous impact and influence on personal meaning and value and the way people act and think.[19] How people answer the big questions impact not only one's view of God, but have a direct impact on how one sees personal and social values, morality, and the meaning of humanity. There are no limits to the reach a person's worldview has. Taking the time to form relationships affords us the ability to understand a person's worldview. Investing in relationships and knowledge of how one sees the world helps to make the space between two people and their ideas a sacred space. A space where Jesus, through the Holy Spirit, can do some work in the lives of people we encounter.

You may not use the worldview questions for every conversation (nor should you), but as you build relationships with others, you should be seeking the answers. In the next two chapters, we will be discussing a practical method for actively building the kinds of relationships that represent the King and His kingdom and lovingly advance the gospel.

CONVERSATION STARTER

The key to understanding others' worldviews is to understand how they answer life's most important questions. However, each of us needs to answer these questions for ourselves as well. Whether you decide to ask in a formal way or an informal conversation, spend time with your students to help them record their answers.

What are your answers to the worldview questions?

CHAPTER FOUR

CREATING RELATIONSHIPS INSTEAD OF CLOSING THE DEAL

I grew up in a great Christian home. I remember Wednesday nights in elementary school. I proudly wore my club shirt decked out with patches boasting verses memorized and tasks completed. One year, I even won the state championship for Pinewood Derby. But more than the accolades and events, I remember hearing the gospel message time and again. While I cannot remember all the vivid details, I do remember accepting Jesus as my savior—several times. Nearly every church event I attended, the gospel message was given. And nearly every time the gospel message was given, I was there raising my hand, accepting Jesus, as if it was the first time all over again. Needless to say, I was missing something.

Even though I accepted Jesus—a lot, I was never discipled. I wasn't mentored. And my earliest understanding of evangelism was all about asking people if they wanted to go to heaven and if so, help them recite a scripted prayer. I was never told anything about liking people or building relationships. To this day, I know very few people who are keen on the idea of Christian evangelism, whether they are Christians or not. Some have no idea what to say, how to say it, or are paralyzed with a fear of saying the wrong thing. Some have had that most memorable experience of the "door-to-door" salesman trying to sell the latest in fire insurance. I am sure they had good intentions and cared enough about spreading the message of Jesus that they were willing to knock door-to-door, but such methods are often unnecessary and ineffective. It is here that an evangelistic effort becomes purely systematic, focused on converts rather than disciples.

Even though these types of situations are often isolated events, evangelism in the western world is centered mainly on more practical, sound bite gospel approaches. The goal is to get as many people converted as possible. There is a fixation with results rather than relationships, getting outcomes rather than proclaiming the gospel. We then run the risk of getting fixated on easy step-by-step methods, sleight-of-hand tricks, and schemes. Success becomes defined as how may prayed a prayer on confessed faith and then it's on to the next person.

Mere numbers, however, does not define success. Sharing the gospel successfully is about obedience, relationships, and discipleship. This is where the practice of good Christian apologetics is not only useful but vital. It is about being a good ambassador for Christ. Meaning you are the best representation of Jesus on earth to those who have never met him. What will they see when they see you? Will you be properly prepared for all the great questions that arise from non-Christians and build lasting and trusting relationships?

YOU CAN'T LEARN TO SWIM ON LAND

In the last chapter, we introduced understanding worldviews as a way to dig deeper into what a person thinks, how they see the world, and why so we can build relationships. Creating healthy cognitive dissonance on key pieces of one's worldview opens doors for new possibilities. We find the fundamental truths of the gospel grounded in relationship—the same relationship God wishes to have with His creation. We can then look for natural avenues for the gospel to make its way into a conversation.

Engaging in long conversations and investing in relationships does, of course, come with risk. What if there is a question you don't have answer for? What if the conversation turns ugly? Wouldn't it be easier just to find ways to present them with a simple gospel message and deal only with those who respond? There is absolutely nothing wrong with just simply showing a person what it means to be saved. That may be your only option. Maybe there is a limited amount of time, and this is the only interaction you will ever have with this particular person. By all means, don't waste time. Make certain they hear the gospel. But whenever and wherever possible, take the time to foster relationships and get to know people. Knowing a little about their background, circumstances, and worldview on a number of topics will build the necessary roads making it easier for the gospel to make its way to their heart and mind.

Don't worry about how prepared you or those you lead, are at first. That will come with time and practice. But the only way to truly learn is to dive in and start talking. Swimmers don't learn to swim on dry land. They can study technique, prepare their bodies by eating right, building muscle, and stretching properly to become better. But the only way to learn to swim is to jump in the water. Theory can only take us so far. We must practice.

QUESTIONS OVER ASSERTIONS

There are, of course, many questions to ask, but what if you find yourself stuck in a conversation or a person has made an assertion that you have trouble responding to? Then you need a way to turn the tables back to them and redirect the conversation. If they make an assertion, you don't need a quick-witted comment to fire back at them. If a person says something offensive to you, there is no need to make a statement, when a simple question will put you right back in control of the conversation and diffuse any potential hostility.

There are also many times you will find yourself trapped. With issues like the problem of evil, morality, same-sex marriage, abortion, and slew of other topics where Christians are often painted as intolerant bigots, you might rather remain mute, than attempt to take a stand. What if you were wrong? What if you don't have all the information? Or become hated as result of the actions and beliefs of others who claim to be Christian, and yet fail to represent Christ?

Then there are those who love the one-liners. The people who would rather not even engage in conversation and just make off-the-cuff statements like, "There are many ways to God, how can you claim only one way?" or, "All Christians are hypocrites," "There are so many contradictions in the Bible it cannot be trusted." Statements like these are often just repeated phrases with no intellectual backing. It is something the person has heard but lacks the research or desire to dig deeper.

So what can you do? How can you advance the conversation in a productive, loving, and relational way? There needs to be a way to continue the conversation, without offending. There needs to be a way to get to the root of a person's belief, but doing so with the very words and attitude of Jesus.

There are three fundamental questions every Christian should be in the habit of asking in every conversation. You will find these questions in a variety of different forms from a variety of different people, but they all get to the same point. First, *"What do you mean by that?"* This question forces the person to clarify broad sweeping statements and assertions. It creates an opportunity for the conversation to go to a deeper level because it forces thinking. Second, *"How did you come to that conclusion?"* This question is considered a clarification question. It encourages people to think what their statement or assertion means underneath the surface. The goal is to create some cognitive dissonance in the person's mind. In other words, allowing the opportunity for doubt to enter their mind. Finally, *"Have you ever considered?"* The first two questions are designed to reveal the holes in another person's worldview. They are meant to locate and reveal the flaws as well as reveal truth. The third question can be used when the opportunity presents itself as a means to introduce the claims of the Christian faith in a non-threatening fashion.

Now imagine having the conversation with the most obscure religion you can think of. In fact, it might be one that either you have zero knowledge of or maybe never even heard of. Do these questions work? A good representative of the gospel of Jesus does not need to know everything about every religion. In fact, a lack of knowledge can be a good thing if you work to ask better questions, however, only if you are humble and teachable. So engaging what you are not familiar with will not faze you because preparedness does not mean an exhaustive knowledge, it simply means having a strategy.

Sticking to asking questions will no doubt open the door to important flaws in their thinking or logic—for example, the absolute truth of the absence of absolute truth. I have had countless conversations with people on the subject of tolerance of every variety. And each time the skeptic, or atheist, humanist, etc. will try to assert that Christians have no business sticking their nose into the lives of others. After all who is to say what is right and wrong, what should or should not be? Of course, this sounds so much like the ideal utopian society. In fact, in sounds perfect. Everyone gets along, and therefore everyone is happy. What might sound good in theory cannot exist in reality. The idea of relative truth is a self-defeating argument. In other words, to say that there is no absolute truth is to deny the premise of the argument of no absolute truth. Therefore the statement in itself is false and defeats the entire argument. A few simple, yet carefully crafted questions will point out these common, yet dangerous flaws in thinking.

THE TASK OF THE APOLOGIST

Even though apologetics is thought of in terms of defense, the task of apologetics should also involve offense. The late R.C. Sproul once wrote that "Apologetics can be used to show that Christianity is true and that all non-Christian worldviews are false."[20] Keep in mind, though, that many other worldviews may contain some truth. For example, there are several worldviews that hold to some sort of creator, the idea of a soul, or life after death. So then, it is true of that worldview when they assert belief in a creator, yet false if and when they deny the creator to be the monotheistic Christian Triune God.

Therefore, our job, through questions and carefully crafted arguments, is to sift through another's assertions, answers, and perceptions to help them understand where their worldview aligns with reality and where it does not; then to present the claims of Christianity in such a way that it connects with the person.

However, even with all of our tactics, techniques, and arguments, people must come first. It can never be about *winning* an argument and adding another notch to our spiritual belt. Our first task is to create relationships with people, connect with them where they are, find common ground and build genuine trust. We want them to understand we value them more than we value convincing them we are right, and they are wrong. Apologetics is about winning souls, not winning arguments. We are not trying to make the other person look stupid, so we can look smarter. Instead, we want to bring them to the conclusion that the only worldview that contains complete truth is the Christian worldview.

We can do this in two very simple ways. First, we can show others that what Christians claim to be true is the best possible explanation for the way things are. In other words, Christianity, given all the evidence, illustrates the absolute truth of reality. Second is relying on God. *Your efforts will never save anyone.* People are only saved by the power of the Holy Spirit of God. Our efforts, we pray, will soften hearts, create doubt, offer a better explanation for a person's existence, and open them up to hear the Gospel of Jesus. Once we do this, our job is done. The rest is in God's hands. We are responsible for our God-given mission and to be stewards of the resources He provides. We may prepare the field, plant the seeds, and even water the crops, but it is God who makes it grow (1 Corinthians 3:7). Apologetics helps us accomplish the tasks God has given each of us by providing for us a confirmation of the truth. Some even call it pre-evangelism—getting a person ready to hear and accept the gospel.

Some, however, often think that to explore the truth claims of the Christian faith, one must abandon his belief or allow dangerous levels of doubt to take over. Contrary to this perception, apologetics does not require abandonment of faith. There is no reason to suspend your beliefs and values to investigate how reasonable it is to have them.[21] But if you're looking for an unbiased approach, you won't find it. You will always look through the lens of the worldview you have until you change your worldview. Therefore if through the efforts of apologetics, we show good reason and argumentation for the truth behind the way things are in this world, we can only enhance our understanding of God, Jesus, and the Christian life. Therefore apologetics does not just defend the Christian worldview—it enhances it, making Christianity consistent with rational and critical thinking.[22]

There are four distinct forms of rational and critical thinking about the Christian worldview which we will need to consider. First, we can give reasons for thinking that the core claims of the Christian worldview are true. Once we consider all the evidence and build a comprehensive case, the Christian worldview continually provides the best answers to life's most significant questions. Second, we can argue that objections against the Christian worldview do not succeed in showing that it is unreasonable or false. These alternative arguments may sound good, but when thoroughly analyzed, they fail to align with reality. Third, we can give reasons for thinking that the claims of worldviews that are logically inconsistent with the Christian worldview are unreasonable or false. In other words, a side-by-side comparison reveals that the Christian worldview remains entirely consistent with itself and its view of the world around us. Finally, we can say that the arguments given for the claims of alternative worldviews inconsistent with Christianity do not succeed in showing that those alternative worldviews are true. What does all this mean? To simplify it, rational and critical thinking about the Christian worldview sharpens our picture of reality, giving us sound reason for thinking that Christianity is true.

WHY THIS APPROACH?

The predominate method of apologetics for students—whether youth group or Christian school is to exclusively focus on worldviews. The assumption is that if you build an understanding of what other people believe, then, you will be able to adequately discuss Christianity as a more sensible alternative. Although this approach has proven useful in some cases, the wide variety of worldviews leaves the Christian student at a significant disadvantage and limits a students effectiveness in sharing their faith.

Instead, we can help students combine the best of both worlds. Students should understand the need to grasp the views of others as well as the diversity of beliefs—even the diversity within a worldview itself. Using the five worldview questions as a means to discover what one's worldview is without any preconceived notions, we can come to an understanding of a person's views beyond the common classifications. This approach also prevents us from judging others or making snap decisions about who someone is or what they believe.

CONCLUSION

C.S. Lewis rightly notes that "we know, in fact, that believers are not cut off from unbelievers by any portentous inferiority of intelligence or any perverse refusal to think. Many of them have been people of powerful minds. Many of them have been scientists. We may suppose them to have been mistaken, but we must suppose that their error was at least plausible."[23]

The goal of the apologist, student or adult, is not to make another look ignorant, to win an argument, or to gain notches in one's proverbial spiritual belt. Even people whom you disagree with may be incredibly smart, articulate, and convinced of what they believe. And most importantly, the people we engage with are people created in the image of God. Our goal is not to have so much knowledge that people look at us as though we think ourselves to be superior, in some way resulting in others believing the way we believe. That is nothing more than arrogance dressed up as truth. Further, our goal is not to learn tricky buzzwords or sly tactics to trick someone into saying something contradictory or circular.

The apologist's goal is simple: to present the best possible case for truth claims of the Christian faith for the benefit of others and the sake of the Kingdom of God. The ultimate goal of the Christian life is to bring the kingdom of heaven to earth and to be the hands and feet of Jesus. Apologetics is meant to accomplish this goal. Apologetics is designed so that you have an opportunity to truly listen in love to understand another person's point of view and to offer them the truth in light of that belief system.

The Apostle John wrote that "If you abide in Jesus, you must walk as he did" (1 John 2:6). For the apologist, developing a relational attitude gives you the opportunity to walk as Jesus did, conversing and accepting the sinners for what and who they are while offering them the truth of the kingdom. Maybe even more so, those we engage with have the opportunity to see the gospel in action. They can see the very image of Jesus within each of us. Of all the tactics, words, and questions you could use, the Jesus in us is by far the most powerful.

Our students place an incredible value on relationships with their peers. They have a desire to love their peers as Jesus did. They want to show grace and mercy. They want to be accepting of all people and are searching desperately to find ways to love, avoid judging, but not condone behaviors that work in contradiction to biblical authority. Apologetics done in relationship provides a marked entrance to the kinds of relationships our students are seeking—the kind of relationships that advance the gospel and glorifies the King.

CONVERSATION STARTER

The key to understanding others' worldviews is to understand how they answer life's most important questions. However, each of us needs to answer these questions for ourselves as well. Whether you decide to ask in a formal way or an informal conversation, spend time with your student to help them record their answers.

What are your answers to the worldview questions?

CHAPTER FIVE

THE ART OF THE ARGUE

If the goal is to merely bring the kingdom of heaven to earth, to talk about Jesus, to be nice to be people, serve them, and care for those who can't care for themselves, then why all this talk about worldview questions and well crafted, purposeful conversations? To some, this could almost seem like a kind of spiritual coercion. We know that it is not us that convince people to believe in Jesus, but the Spirit who convicts people. But God has chosen His people to play a part in how He reaches the lost. And even from the days of the early church, disciples of Jesus have worked hard to engage people on an academic level using sound logic and flawless argumentation.

WHY LOGIC AND ARGUING

Why in the world would we speak of things like logic when following Jesus is all about your heart? There is often a sort of false understanding of logic, its use and purpose; especially in the Christian world. Logic is often viewed as cold, calculated, and void of any emotional significance. Add logic to matters of faith, and you may find yourself accused of selling the gospel short of its transformational power and its strong emotional ties to humanity's heart condition. Most of Western

Christianity is highly emotional and therefore often shuns any intellectual discipline that assists in furthering the gospel. When Christians usually consider the idea of logic the predominant thought is a cold science and therefore not needed in the world of faith.

We need a means to think clearly and redemptively so that we can carefully reason (or be logical) about what we believe and why. Once again, let's return to what Peter told his audience:

> "But in your hearts revere Christ as Lord. Always be prepared to give an answer to everyone who asks you to give the reason for the hope that you have. But do this with gentleness and respect, keeping a clear conscience, so that those who speak maliciously against your good behavior in Christ may be ashamed of their slander." -1 Peter 3:15-16

So beyond the usual call in apologetics to be ready at any moment to give a defense for what you believe and why, Peter is making it clear here that our emotions are tied to our reasoning. When we rely on emotions, we risk it becoming the dominant means of thinking and reasoning or more commonly, letting our emotions "get the best of us." Thus we allow for critical errors in reasoning known as logical fallacies (which we look at later).

UNDERSTANDING LOGIC & LOGICAL FALLACY

So then, what do we mean by logic? Is there such a thing as a Christian view of logic? The basic idea behind logic is determining what is true and how we know what is, or is not true. It is logic that helps keep our assertions grounded in reality instead of fanciful idealism. This is done primarily through a formal system of reasoning. For the follower of Jesus, the search for what is true and how we can know it is always about what we know (and how we can know) about God and the Bible. Within the world of academia, there is a system of academic arguments, persuasion, even misdirection, and coercion.

However, logical arguments and purposeful fallacies are used in all kinds of professions. For example, the world of sales, in some cases will use logical fallacies, persuasion, and emotion to make a sale. Or consider politics. Politicians regularly commit common logical fallacies purposefully to bring down their political opponent and advance their agenda. It will, of course, be our goal to assert good arguments that can help to lead us to a wise conclusion and consequently steer clear of logical fallacies—steering clear of argumentation that may sound plausible but that uses tricks or gimmicks rather than solid reasoning. Its goal is to distract or lead a person from the reality of truth. One might commit a fallacy on purpose or without even realizing it.

So let's look at some of the most common logical fallacies.

Ad Hominem. Attacking someone's character rather than their argument. This happens more often than you might think. Think of the last political debate you listened to or watched. How often did the candidates spend more time hurling insults at each other rather than talk about the issues? President, Donald Trump is masterful at this. If he does not want to deal with an issue, he uses insults to distract the listeners and changes the focus of their attention to their character.

Anytime a person goes after character, purposefully avoiding the issue or argument at hand, is speaking ad hominem.

Straw Man. When you think of a straw man, think of a scarecrow. These are "fake" people, made of straw designed to scare away crows and other birds that could potentially eat or harm a crop. It is not real but made to look real. The same goes for a straw man argument. For example, "I don't believe in God because I hate the idea of a mean grandfather in the sky, with rods of lightning, waiting to strike us down." If that were who God was, I wouldn't believe in him either. But this line of reasoning builds up a false conception of something, for the sole purpose of knocking it down. Or more formally, stating the argument of your opponent in a way, they wouldn't have said it. This could be done intentionally to make your case appear stronger, or unintentionally due to a lack of knowledge.

False Analogy. "An argument from analogy where the analogy does not result in appropriate parallels."[24] Essentially this fallacy combines the power of analogy and hyperbole and infuses it inappropriately into an argument.

Slippery Slope. This line of argument tries to show someone that if they take a first step, they will find themselves unavoidably heading in the direction of embracing an unavoidable consequence.[25] In other words, asserting that allowing homosexuals to marry logically leads to allowing people to marry their dog. However, it is important to note that what might appear to simply be ridiculous and unimaginable, could be a skillful move to shift the burden of proof to one's opponent.

Confusion equals Cause. This is something Christians and non-Christians are guilty of on a regular basis. Rather than search for a legitimate reason or cause of something we quantify our confusion by placing a sort of blanket statement either giving credit to God or implicating Him. For Christians, this often appears in the form of using God as the end all explanation for anything unexplained. Conversely, non-Christians quickly will implicate God. This is especially evident when talking about the problem of evil and suffering.

Argument from Authority. Think back to when you were a kid. Think of a time when you entered into an argument with one of your friends. You, of course, are convinced of your opinion, and your friend is, of course, equally convinced of his. You have no proof or authority in which to back your position—mostly because in fifth grade you don't realize that is necessary. So you toss out the most logical statement you can think of. "Because my mom told me so!" What better source of authority. Arguing solely from authority is a relatively weak position. Even stating to a non-Christian that you believe something because "God says so," only takes you so far in the conversation. It may hold water in like company, but to the skeptic, it means very little.

Fallacy of False Cause. This assumes a connection between two things based on temporal or accidental connections.[26] Superstition among athletes commits this common fallacy. Assuming that a certain pair of socks, or shirt, or pre-game ritual has some direct causation to winning a game based exclusively on the coincidence that the team won a game and you happened to be wearing that pair of socks or went through a particular pre-game routine. This is also commonly called the fallacy of *post hoc, ergo propter hoc* (Latin for "after this, therefore, on account of this).

Argument by Consensus. I remember growing up listening to my mom continually asking me if all my friends jumped off a bridge, would I? That question was essentially a reminder from her that I was committing the fallacy of argument by consensus. To put the fallacy much more simply, "everyone's doing it!" If 90% of people purchased a particular brand that does not necessarily mean it is the best brand. Advertisers may use a statistic like this to claim a product's superiority, but the reality may be that the product is terrible.

False Dilemma. Giving two extremes as the only alternatives to a position, when there are multiple positions. Claiming that, "If you don't believe hell is eternal for everyone, you're a universalist." Or, "If you oppose the transgender bathroom laws, then you are a bigot."

The difference between logic in the secular world and the Christian world is that as followers of Jesus wisdom is ultimately derived from God. Sin hinders our ability to reason correctly and consistently and even our ability to interpret the Bible. Our sin nature has within it the desire to be autonomous, and it affects our reasoning. But it is the renewal of the mind that changes things and therefore affects how truth is perceived. Naturally, non-Christians suppress the fact that they are receiving truth from God, and that what they know is found first of all in the mind of God.

CRAFTING A LOGICAL ARGUMENT

So then what are the elements of a properly and well-crafted logical argument? The basic structures of an argument are the premises and the conclusion. The premises are the facts of the matter: The statements that you know (or strongly believe) to be true. Ideally, these statements are provable or strongly considered to be true based on the amount and degree of evidence presented. In many cases, however, an argument also includes intermediate steps that show how the premises lead incrementally to that conclusion. Finally, is the conclusion—this is the outcome of your argument. If you've written the intermediate steps in a clear progression, the conclusion should be fairly obvious.

Take a look at the example below.

Premise 1: Caffeine is considered an addictive substance

Premise 2: Kozak drinks coffee every day

Premise 3: All coffee has some caffeine in it

Conclusion: Therefore, Kozak is probably addicted to caffeine

Based on medical data and research, I can make a strong case for premise one. Caffeine is an addictive substance. This is a great way to begin any proof; provide some information or statement that is nearly impossible to refute. Premise two begins to state the case in a more direct manner. If I am trying to prove how much I am addicted to coffee, then I, at some point, will need to make a provable statement concerning my coffee consumption. Clearly, how much coffee I drink is observable and provable.

Premise three then connects the two previous statements together. To show that I am addicted to caffeine, I need to show that caffeine is addictive, I drink coffee, coffee has caffeine, and so forth. Premise three bridges that gap. Which then leads to a natural conclusion. I am, therefore, addicted to caffeine. What you should notice here is the logical flow from one statement to the other which then formulates a natural conclusion based on the data presented. If I am missing any one of these premises, I am in danger of committing a logical fallacy.

CONCLUSION

When we speak of arguments in an academic setting, we are not at all talking about picking fights with people in hopes to win an argument so we can boast in our abilities or feel good about ourselves. Arguments are designed to be well crafted logical trains of thought that assist in coming to a truthful conclusion and explaining how we came to a particular conclusion and why it makes more sense than some other particular alternative.

Paul was logical; Peter was logical, even Jesus crafted logical arguments. God gave us the ability to reason from the Scriptures how Jesus is the means by which we can experience God and enter His kingdom. Crafting well-organized logical arguments allows Christians to compete successfully in the marketplace of ideas.

CONVERSATION STARTER

Communication is a two-way street. Both speaker and listener have a responsibility to communicate as efficiently as possible. However, often our only goal is to be right no matter the consequence—even if to make our point we must stray from logic.

What logical fallacies can you and your students pick up on in each other's everyday conversations?

THE ART OF THE ARGUE

CHAPTER SIX
FAITH AND REASON

During my high school and college years, I considered the idea of God or Jesus with a heavy dose of skepticism. I not only held to the belief that Jesus could not be God; I doubted whether he was even a real person. I considered Jesus to be more of an ideology or creedal declaration. When life spun out of control, when it could not be explained, or when all else seemed unreasonable, faith in Jesus was my substitute for common sense. Jesus served a purpose. He was the rabbit's foot, the bandage, and the duct tape solution until I could figure out how to fix things myself. When something was broken, faith in Jesus was the crutch to use until I was healed.

This was how I thought faith worked. A belief that defied common sense, lacked proof, and was completely illogical. Incidentally, this idea of faith is exactly what made it so easy for me to leave Jesus behind. If I cannot see God, then how could I have any proof of Him? If I lack the proof, then clearly believing in such a thing is not all that far from believing in Santa Claus, the Tooth Fairy or the Easter Bunny. I have never witnessed the appearance of any of these childhood figures so, as I grew older, common sense led me to the natural conclusion that, despite my parent's insistence, these myths were nothing more than popular social conventions. So we end up championing faith against reason as the thing you can have when evidence is lacking. Faith, we are told is supposed to fill the holes in our arguments. So, for the Christian, it seems that when one cannot produce evidence for the resurrection, for the existence of God, etc., a blind, uninformed faith fills the void. It might look good, but lacks any structural integrity or intellectual honesty.

Whether we like it or not, our students are missing the point of faith and treating Jesus more like they would Santa Claus. Many lack the proper framework in which to build their faith on. Then we, as leaders, wonder why students continue to see Jesus as irrelevant and unnecessary.

GETTING CLARITY ON FAITH

I have heard even the most committed Christians talk as though strong faith was an ample substitution for convincing reasons or evidence. But if apologetics is suggesting that there are legitimate reasons to believe in Jesus, or have faith in him, then it would seem we disagree about the nature of faith. Faith according to one dictionary definition is listed as, "belief that is not based on proof."[27] The famous atheistic philosopher Friedrich Nietzsche commented that "At times one remains faithful to a cause only because its opponents do not cease to be insipid." But, maybe more than these, is how faith is viewed on a popular level. The classic Christmas movie, *Miracle on 34th Street*, teaches that "Faith is believing in something when common sense tells you not to."[28]

If these examples have any accuracy, then faith in Jesus Christ is nothing more than blind trust in something based on no proof or reason whatsoever. But, this distinction does not end with a disagreement between the Christian and the skeptic. Even in Christian circles, faith and its relationship to reason come under fire on a regular basis. While many view faith to be a clear compliment to reason—that Christians have reasons for faith in Jesus—others view matters of faith and reason to be separate spheres of one's life. Each has a role but does not tread outside that role. Still, there are Christians who go so far as to say that faith is antithetical to reason and that the two have no business commingling. There is an apparent fear associated with reasoning in matters of faith. However, in spite of objections to the contrary, faith, and reason are not opposites that refuse to exist in the same space in time. It is not as though having faith means that you are publicly declaring war on reason. They are not at all mutually exclusive. In fact, they are the perfect compliment. I might even go so far as to say that, within the Christian worldview, they are dependent on each other.

But, in large part, the intensity between faith and reason stems from the vast amount of varying definitions of faith. It seems as though this simple little word, already packed with incredible significance and meaning, is pulled and twisted to make faith look like reason's little brother. In other words, you might have faith, but someday, when you grow up and get big and smart, you can have reason. Twentieth-century American journalist and critic of almost everything, H.L. Mencken, went so far as to claim that faith in God is not only unreasonable but evidence of an incurable disease.

> "Faith may be defined briefly as an illogical belief in the occurrence of the improbable. Or, psychoanalytically, as a wish neuroses. There is thus a flavor of the pathological in it; it goes beyond the normal intellectual process and passes into

the murky domain of transcendental metaphysics. A man full of faith is simply one who lost (or never had) the capacity for clear and realistic thought. He is not a mere ass: he is actually ill. Worse, he is incurable, for disappointment, being essentially an objective phenomenon, cannot permanently affect his subjective infirmity. His faith takes on the virulence of a chronic infection. What he usually says, in substance, is this: 'Let us trust in God, *who has always fooled us in the past.*'"[29]

So, in light of these varied definitions, we need to reconstruct what Christians mean when we talk about faith. Then, we can see if faith in Jesus has any merit to be grounded in reason. This way, when we, and those we are leading, speak of faith, we can be sure that our definition is the same as the person with whom we are talking to.

TOWARD A DEFINITION OF FAITH

If faith believes in something despite common sense, then belief in Jesus is ridiculous—unless, of course, faith is about what we know as an extension of what we have experienced. The disciples, and many others in the early church had faith in Jesus and saw and experienced him. Even more than that, many witnessed and experienced his resurrection. So, what did they have faith in? Certainly, common sense told them that Jesus, who was once dead, is now alive. So, faith in what? The disciples' faith was their certainty that, in Jesus, God has fulfilled all that He had promised from the beginning and their hope that His promise would be carried through to the end (Habakkuk 2:4; Matthew 8:4-6; Philippians 3:9; Hebrews 11). Their faith in Jesus rested in the covenant faithfulness of God. It is not as if God sticks you in a dark room, blindfolded, and at the highest point from a ladder tells you to jump into an unknown black abyss. And somehow, because He is God, we are just supposed to trust blindly and jump, risking life and limb, and think nothing of it. If this were true, then the skeptics would have the upper hand, and I would agree with them. What reason would I have in jumping? Instead, God turns the lights on, shows us the plan, tells us to jump, but then shows us how we are going to fly. I know that He will come through because He has shown me all the times that He has come through throughout history.

The self-authenticating witness of the Holy Spirit reveals God's active involvement in history.[30] We know Christianity to be true and our faith in Jesus to be grounded in such truth because the Spirit tells us. We can stand in the room on the ladder with all the knowledge in the world about God's plan and purpose because the Spirit has revealed those things to us. It is only by the Spirit that we *know* Christianity to be true. To put this simply, when we are indwelled with the Spirit (i.e., become a believer in Jesus Christ), we are given the revelation and knowledge of the truth, as a result of the Spirit's work (Col. 2:2; 1 Thess. 1:5; 1 John 3:24, 4:13).

In his first letter, the Apostle John frequently uses his characteristic phrase, "by this we know" (1 John 2:3, 3:16, 24; 4:6, 13, 5:2), to emphasize that, as Christians, we have a confident knowledge that our faith is true, that we really do abide in God, and that God really does live in us. We would call this a properly basic or foundational belief. A belief that is properly basic is one that does not require any other belief to function as the foundation. We cannot prove it because it is foundational and no one can deny it.

For the unbeliever, the Spirit's ministry is one of conviction and conversion—convicting the unbeliever of his sin, of God's righteousness, and of his condemnation before God. Man alone is an enemy of God and does not seek God on his own, nor does he understand spiritual things (Rom. 3:10-11). No one fails to become a Christian because of the lack of good reasons to do so, but he fails because he loves the darkness and wants nothing to do with God. However, the unbeliever who is truly seeking God will become convinced of the truth of the Christian message. This is the work of the Holy Spirit and where reason alone will no doubt fail. Reason cannot create faith, but reason can provide sufficient evidence for the existence of God, which is the logical conclusion of faith. According to theologian and apologist, Norman Geisler, "Reason inquires about what is to be believed before it believes in it."[31]

But, how does faith work with reason? How, then, can we determine what to believe in and what not to believe in? In order to nail down an accurate definition of faith, we first need to understand its relationship to reason.

THE RELATIONSHIP BETWEEN FAITH AND REASON

Faith absent reason—matters of faith are private, and matters of reason are public. This means that one does not mix the worlds of faith and reason. This might be the case for a person studying the field of science. A scientist can deduce, via reason, a particular conclusion based on fact. Conversely, faith would be a private aspect, inner morality, or a blind vote of confidence. Can this view fit into our Christian mindset?

Faith against reason—reason has no place in spiritual matters. In this view, a person cannot reason about matters of faith—this is called *fide-ism*, a view that is held by many Christians. If this is true, then how then can we determine what to believe in and what not to believe in? If fideism offers no reason, then why should we choose this system over any other system? With every belief comes a reason to choose that belief. Therefore, fideism is a self-defeating argument, in other words, the conclusion of the argument defeats its own premise. For example, if I walked up to you on the street and announced "I do not exist," it immediately becomes clear that my premise—I do not ex-ist—is defeated by the conclusion—the fact that I am standing in front of you telling you that I do not exist. If you maintain a particular be-lief, you must have a reason, even if the reason is ridiculous.

Faith and reason—each has a role, and they compliment each other. Faith is personal trust in something or someone—in this case, Jesus Christ. There are also convincing reasons to trust God; some will trust Him, others will not. However, God has provided all the reasons in the world to have faith in the promises He has made to His people. "Christians study the Bible and discuss it and that we seek to under-stand how the Bible applies to our lives shows that we attempt to un-derstand (reason) what we believe (faith). Reason does not cause faith, but our faith is not unreasonable."[32]

Faith and reason should never be classified as two pieces of our lives that are independent of each other. God has provided humanity with the ability to think, reason, invent and create. Our job, as people created in the image of God, is to use the brains that God gave us to enhance our understanding of who He is and what His mission is (i.e., Christian faith).

FAITH AND ITS PROPER RELATIONSHIP TO REASON

So, is it better to believe something despite what our common sense tells us? Maybe, the dictionary's definition of faith is correct, or the conversation between mom and daughter in *Miracle on 34th Street* was accurate after all? But, then faith would be nothing more than religious experience, which, in reality, has only subjective value when confronted with an opposing worldview. In his book, *Love the Lord With All Your Mind,* J.P. Moreland defines faith as, "that which is reasonable to believe." So then, what makes faith reasonable? Further, what takes my faith beyond its existential reality and to be more reasonable that another's? Let's take another look at Thomas, one of the original twelve disciples, for example.

I can imagine the stress of the events leading up to the crucifixion, the danger that inevitably threatened him, and, undoubtedly, several other factors caused doubt to creep into his mind. The idea of resurrection proved to be too much for him. So, Jesus gave Thomas a clear *reason* to believe by showing him the wounds in his hands and side. What more reason would Thomas need? Thomas emphatically declares, "My Lord and my God" (John 20:27-28). At that moment it did not matter what Thomas may or may not have known to be true, he needed someone to *show* him what was true. This is the role of reason.

If the Holy Spirit plays the main role in giving us the fundamental knowledge of Christianity's truth, then argument and evidence serve as supporting roles. Reason cannot serve as a basis for belief but can serve as a tool to help us better understand and defend our faith. Truth can be known whether or not there are reasons. However, as William Lane Craig points out, "The role of rational argumentation in knowing Christianity to be true is the role of a servant. A person knows Christianity to be true because the Holy Spirit tells him it is true, and while arguments and evidence can be used to support this conclusion, they cannot legitimately overrule it."[33]

The disciples were reminded to have faith that Jesus would remain with them through the Holy Spirit. Based on the post-resurrected appearances of Jesus, it is safe to say that the disciples had ample reason to believe. Thomas may have needed evidence, but so did Peter, John, and many others. Jesus ate with his disciples, walked along the Emmaus road with two disciples and even appeared to more than five hundred people before ascending to heaven. And it was not until Thomas placed his hands into the nail pierced wrists of Jesus that he declared Jesus as Lord.

Christianity is based on truth and, in itself, contains all that is true. Therefore, based on evidence, we would say that we know Christianity is true and, therefore is reasonable to believe. For example, take a look at Exodus 8-11. God provides more than sufficient reason for Pharaoh and Moses to believe not only who God is, but also how He will rescue His people. After this, God commands the nation of Israel to remember all that God had done for them. They were to remember the covenant. Each time Israel looked back, either through story, festival or the practice of the Law, there were reasons for Israel to believe that God is and would continue to be faithful to His covenant. Essentially, they had reasons to believe and reason to have faith.

Over and over, Israel, the prophets, kings, soldiers, the disciples and the early church consistently asked, prayed for and consequently were given ample reasons to believe that God was exactly who He said He was and that His promises would always stand. Instead of separating faith and reason, we see that through Scripture and God's created order, He has given us every reason to believe in the promise revealed in Jesus.

FAITH

Faith is not wishful thinking, nor a blind trust fall. Faith is about hope. Faith is being sure of what we hope for, and certain of we do not see (Hebrews 11:1). According to the writer of Hebrews, faith rests in certainty. Believers in Jesus are sure of hope; hope that what God has promised in the past is made known and fulfilled in Jesus in the present and will be made known in full in the New Heavens and New Earth. It is through God's covenant faithfulness that Christians can trust that what God has promised will indeed come. In short, because Jesus resurrected and defeated death, followers of Jesus can be certain of the same future. Although we do not see God physically, He has provided all the certainty and reason we need to trust or have faith in Him.

CONCLUSION

It is distressing to think that people all around the world, especially in our western culture, are learning that faith is a hindrance to real intellect; or something used as a substitute, something for the weak-minded, something that lacks common sense, or worse, something that is equated to an incurable disease. What the skeptic does not realize is that without faith, of any kind, it is almost impossible to function in the everyday world. How would you go to sleep at night without having anxiety about whether or not your house is going to cave in on you, or that someone is going to sneak in at night and rob you? How would you get in your car and drive down the road without believing that oncoming traffic won't suddenly veer into your lane and strike you head on? I know this sounds a bit depressing, but think of the countless ways we have faith that this or that is not going to happen to us. Why do we believe that, more often than not, life will carry on as usual? Because we base our trust or faith on the reasons we have for doing so, the more reasons that we discover, the more faith that we have.

CONVERSATION STARTER

As I am sure you have noticed, faith—especially among Christians—is often misunderstood or incorrectly defined. Before any meaningful conversations about faith occur, we need to be sure that those we lead are entirely clear about what mean when we speak of faith.

How does faith (in anything) affect the way you live? How does (or should) faith in Christ affect the way you live?

CHAPTER SEVEN
DISCOVERING TRUTH

What would say if I told you that my iPhone brought me great joy and happiness? What if I told you that every time I picked it up, sent someone a text, checked my email, or scrolled through my social media news feed, I felt a rush of adrenaline that sent me into a state of euphoria? Now I know what your thinking, "This guy has a serious problem." But all judgments aside, is my statement about my phone true? What if you disagreed with me? What if you asserted that personal devices of any kind are destructive and should never be used? Is that a true statement? The interesting reality here is that both of these statements can be true for both of us at the same time and in the same place—even when they completely contradict. But how is that possible? Before I answer that, let's consider another statement about the same phone.

What would you say if I told you that my iPhone enabled me to avoid getting the flu each year? Simply by engaging in the regular operation of the multitude of functions on my phone, I can completely avoid contracting the influenza virus. Now I am no longer just addicted to my phone, I have gone completely crazy. Why? Because that statement is ridiculous. One could easily prove that there is absolutely no correlation between getting the flu and using a cell phone. So how is it that we can easily say the second statement is false, but the first statement—although contradictory views exist—is absolutely true?

FACT VS. FEELING

These two statements are simply the difference between what is fact and what is feeling—what is objective and what is subjective. And to have the appropriate conversation about truth we need to first understand the difference. My first statement about my phone bringing me happiness was a statement describing a personal preference. The statement was about how I *feel* about my phone. No different than a preference for a particular food or in movies.

For example, I am a huge Marvel movie lover. So naturally, I tend to think that movies like *Captain America* or *Avengers* are the best movies. However, you may despise superhero movies but love romantic comedies. So in this case what is true for you and what is true for me can be entirely different, but equally true. We might disagree on movie choices, but in the end, we graciously respect each other's views. Maybe even see each other's movies. In some cases, this poses no problems at all. How we feel about movies can be equally true for each of us. We call this subjective truth. The nature of truth revolves around or speaks to the subject. In this case, I am the subject. The nature of truth is entirely dependent on my preference and depends on my interaction with the statement in question.

However, my second statement is not about me but my phone. I was making a statement about the nature of my phone—a statement that could be verified with objective facts. So the truth (or untruth) of a statement has nothing to do with me or my opinion. Just because I think my phone has medicinal powers does not make it true. For example, what if I told you that sitting here next to me was a cup of coffee? If you were in the same room as me while I type this, you would agree this is an objectively true statement. Meaning my thoughts or feelings on the matter have no bearing on the reality that here next to me is a cup of coffee.

These statements have nothing to do with me, but with the objects I am describing. In other words, my statement about a cup of coffee is true regardless if you had never seen or had a cup of coffee; true even if you had no taste buds. True, even if, based on your limited or lack of exposure to coffee, you had devised a different name, and created a different purpose. The fact of the matter is that the cup of coffee would remain a cup of coffee until it is no longer a cup of coffee and no longer possess the properties that make it a cup of coffee. The cup of coffee can never be beer, water, or a Diet Pepsi. It's a cup of coffee. Objective truth doesn't care about opinion, feelings, experiences, or preferences, only what matches reality.

Subjective truth has more to do with opinion, and objective truth concerns facts. Subjective means something is true based on how you or I might feel about something. Objective bases truth claims off of the validity of the evidence. So whether or not I like the color red is just as true that your favorite color is blue. However, whether or not I can bench press 350 pounds can easily be tested by letting me try. If I do it, it's true; if I drop the weight on my face, then it is false.

IDEAS HAVE CONSEQUENCES

But what happens when we start talking about things like morality, differing worldviews, and religions? What happens if I throw the Bible and Jesus into the mix? If we stick to a postmodern way of seeing the world through the lens of subjectivism, objective truth is tossed out with the rest of the outdated cultural fads we once knew and loved. So for the Christian, when we say such outlandish things like, Jesus' brash statement, "I am the way, the truth and the life, no one gets to the Father, except through me" (John 14:6), people are outraged and Christians are reduced to exclusive unloving, unaccepting, bigots. After all, no one worldview can claim they have the true account of reality. Communities, ethnic groups, genders, and other contingent factors should determine truth.[34]

Like it or not, we live in a world that considers it a virtue to deny the existence of truth. However, there was a time when truth was sacred, valued, and embraced. It was considered the independent standard by which we measured our existence within reality. Truth is now under fire. Our students are being indoctrinated into a worldview daily in the classroom, through music, movies, television, and even politics. A worldview taught as something intimately connected with one's experience. Truth is what you make of it. It can be different for different people; change based on current moods, and desired lifestyles. As a result, we have created a space that allows for opposing beliefs to own equal strands of truth. We call this cultural relativism. Simply put, culture decides moral norms, beliefs, values, and practices of culture—culture defines truth for itself.

Everywhere we look there are subtle (and some not-so-subtle) references to relativism. Think about what some of the most prominent people in media offer as pearls of wisdom to the rest of us commoners.

"There's no right or wrong, success or failure." - Miley Cyrus

"You know, I just do whatever feels right to me! And so that's what you're gonna get!" - Bruno Mars

"Have it your way." - Burger King

"Speaking your truth is your most powerful tool we have." – Oprah Winfrey

These are just a few of hundreds of examples of Hollywood personalities, politicians, sports stars, and educators expounding personalized morality, and an "everyone has a piece of truth" mentality all drawn from a rejection of absolute truth.

In one sense, this kind of thinking seems perfectly harmless. In some ways, it almost sounds utopic. Everyone gets along, and no one is ever wrong. But for this to happen religious views that claim to possess truth or that seem intolerant of competing views must not enter public discourse for fear that disagreement may appear to be hateful. Views regarding personal or religious beliefs once discussed and debated in the town square have now been quarantined to one's personal space. Pushing your beliefs on anyone else will not be tolerated for any reason.

Think of it as a two-story house. In most homes in western culture, the living area, the kitchen, and the dining area are considered the more public place of the home. When visitors stop by, you usually congregate in one of those areas—the kitchen being often where the closest of friends gather. However, the bedrooms on the second floor are the private space. It is a place the general public does not see. The world's view on sharing what we think and feel is much like this two-story house. The public space downstairs is our public sphere, the place where we might share culture's accepted norms, agreeable thoughts on things like politics, justice, or family. However our thoughts and opinions on religion—especially as it relates to truth—remains upstairs in the sacred sphere of life. Opinions here are meant—even demanded—to be kept private, as sharing may offend. Incidentally, we have allowed relativism to become the accepted norm when we consider the nature of truth.

So can more than one truth exist in the same space and time like most seem to claim? Can two competing truths co-exist? Is it possible that relativism can rightly claim the absence of absolute objective truth with absolute certainty? Or, is the claim of subjective, or relative truth, an objective claim itself?

When we try to put relativism into practice, we will inevitably come up empty-handed. For example, consider the following statement: "No sentences are longer than six words." We call a sentence like this self-refuting. The outcome of the statement refutes it's own premise. In other words, the sentence, "no sentences are longer than six words" has in its sentence, seven words. Just like my grandma used to say, "never say never." Although it may be sound wisdom from a loving grandma, it nevertheless refutes itself.

It is these kinds of statements that we regularly ascribe to truth. I can't tell you how many times I have people tell me that there is no absolute truth. I typically respond by asking them if they are absolutely sure. The statement, "there is no absolute truth," just like grandma's never say never, is self-refuting. Absolute certainty that absolute truth doesn't exist is, in itself an absolute statement about what is, or is not, true.

If the logic behind relative truth is permitted, then we inevitably violate the Law of Non-Contradiction, which states that something cannot be both truth and not true at the same time. So either you are reading this page or not, I can lift 350 pounds or not, I am drinking coffee or not, or Jesus is the way, the truth, and the life, or he is not. Statements about truth are statements about reality. Our goal in discovering what is true is discovering a matching relationship between a thought and reality.[35]

COMPETING CLAIMS OF TRUTH

Take a minute and think back to the time when you were a child, and you were absolutely certain that Santa Claus, the white-bearded man who rode into town on a sleigh pulled by eight reindeer, climbed down your chimney and left you presents on Christmas Eve, but only if you had been good all year long and were asleep when he arrived. For many of us, Santa Claus was a significant part of our reality. Maybe your parents took you to the mall to visit him. If you're like me, you were a Santa Claus evangelist and, when necessary, an apologist for the North Pole. It is only a matter of time before you realize that there is no sleigh, no reindeer, no red coat, no white beard, and certainly no chimney sweeping. Some of that perceived "magic" of Christmas is lost when you discover that the presents are from your parents. But, why do we believe this to be true for so long? Why do our parents let us believe it for so long? And how is it that we come to know the "truth" that Santa Claus is not real.

For many, Santa Claus, the Easter Bunny, or any other figure created from social convention does two specific things. First, it seems coherent. Mom and dad patch the holes, make sure stories are as consistent as possible, and make sure that the idea of Santa might just be possible. Second, belief serves a practical purpose. Simply put, be good, and get presents. To get a better idea of what I mean, take a minute and make the most coherent and logical case for Santa Claus that you can. Make it as convincing of an argument as possible.

Making a coherent and logical case for something is known as the Coherence View of Truth—truth consists in its belonging to a coherent, consistent, or unified set of beliefs.[36] In other words, as long as the belief is consistent and makes sense, it can be considered true. So when we consider belief in Santa, the Easter Bunny, or the Tooth Fairy—over the course of time, the belief system of each has been created to be coherent and consistent. For example, I remember reading as a kid that Santa came down a chimney. However, my problem was that my house did not have a chimney. So naturally, I asked my mom to explain this apparent inconsistency in the story. To make sure I maintained my belief in Santa Claus, she explained the mode by which Santa came into the house. The explanation was consistent, logical (for a child) and coherent. What could be wrong with this? Fantasies can be coherent, but not true. Regarding Christianity, the skeptic might be able to make a coherent case that Jesus is not God, but merely a man.

If I try hard enough, I can make an argument for Santa Claus, even taking care of some contradictions. As long as it is coherent (for the most part), then I can claim it as true. The bottom line is that this view can lead to many possible truths, as long as it seems consistent and logical. So, when the kid who firmly believes in Santa encounters another who firmly denies Santa, one view must be correct and the other incorrect. No level of love or tolerance can prove otherwise.

What if we defined truth as something that serves a useful purpose? Add a component to your proof of Santa Claus that shows the usefulness of your belief. The Pragmatic View of truth states that truth is that which is useful or that works or contributes to human well-being. The potential problems are much the same. Again, this view can lead to contradictory views being true, because they are useful. Finding something useful could be different for each person, leading to relativism or the lack of absolute truth. Something could be true and completely worthless, just as there can be useful, false beliefs.

You may remember that, as a child, belief in Santa Claus, though sometimes far-fetched, served an incredibly useful purpose, like receiving presents, candy, etc. After all, why would you risk the presents? At that time, it served your best interest to continue to believe, regardless of the reality. However, one's belief in Santa, regardless of how coherent and practical it sounded as a child will eventually give way to reality.

What we believe must align itself with reality for it to be true. We call this The Correspondence Theory of Truth, meaning truth is that which corresponds to reality. If we were to make the statement that the sky is blue, that statement or belief could only be true if it corresponds to reality. In other words, I can look up and see that on a cloudless day the sky is indeed blue. Therefore, the statement is true. Coherence and practicality is merely providing opinion—which may or may not contain truth

For example, if a professional football team went undefeated throughout the season, made its way through the playoffs and into the Super Bowl; it could be said that the team is the best in football and consequently will win the championship game. However, this assertion is not up to you. The belief is formed, but the outcome is yet to be determined. Therefore, regardless of what you hope for, or what you perceive, the outcome of game is determined by reality (i.e., the reality that the team either won or lost and is therefore either the best team in the league or not). You do not have the luxury of picking what is true or what corresponds with reality.

So when we are talking about faith in Christ as something that is true, we are doing more than offering our opinion or one of several religious options. We are offering a worldview system that we claim corresponds with reality. When we say that Jesus is the only means of salvation, we are saying that anything else that offers salvation of another kind is false. Therefore, if the Christian worldview claims to hold what is absolutely true, than anything that runs contrary must then be false. But this is where Christians often find themselves entrenched in a battle they cannot win against the rest of the world.

ON THE FRONTLINES

For the first time in U.S. history, students are growing up in a post-Christian culture. The largest and fastest growing religious identity is now the *nones*—those who pledge no religious affiliation. And according to Barna research the younger the generation, the more post-Christian it becomes.[37] Students of Generation Z are confronted with issues earlier generations never imagined. Many of them are standing at the crossroads between a church that appears completely out of touch with culture and a world pressuring them to conform to twenty-first century social norms of relativism and postmodern thinking.

Supporters of a reality based on relativism continue to assert that; "truth is not determined by its connection to objective reality but by various social constructions devised for different purposes." [38] Meaning that because our world has so many different cultures, contexts, and religions, truth is just a social construct created differently by each culture, therefore explaining reality very differently, and therefore allowing for multiple versions of truth. But as we will see in the chapters to follow, allowing ourselves and our cultures to serve as the standard for assessing reality is not only impossible but also dangerous. The claim that there is no objective reality is a claim about reality and, therefore, objective. If indeed reality is up to the individual or culture, then what happens when tolerance can no longer bridge the gap between differing opinions? For example, we might say that objective moral standards might regard things like rape, incest, murder, and terrorist attacks as evil. But what happens when we stand firm on the grounds of no objective truth? How can I know that such things are evil, and how can I even claim that they are evil without becoming oppressive and intolerant myself?

Relativism, on the surface, looks very much like a loving, tolerant, peaceful, all accepting way of living. But, without an objective standard in which to test against reality, we are left with nothing more than a mere opinion that will no doubt change based on the latest trends, politicians, or Hollywood personalities. We are left with personal judgments and subjective claims that, when they collide, will cause more harm and division than the harmony and love much of our world is seeking.

On September 22, 1987, aired the first episode of the soon to be hit series *Full House*. Although the storyline differed slightly from the norm, the show boasted traditional family values, no sexual content, and no political or social agendas. It was a show the entire family could enjoy without fear of filtering inappropriate content. Only seven years later we were introduced to *Friends*. For ten years the world sat for thirty minutes a week to watch our culture transform before our eyes. This story of six friends in their twenty-somethings made pre-marital sex, homosexuality, excessive drinking, and the refusal to grow up acceptable in western culture. Television and media continued pushing the envelope opening the doors for show's like the 2016 Net-flix production, *13 Reasons Why*. A show that was widely popular among students that normalized the display of things like rape, suicide, pornography, and issues of gender identity—and all, on demand. Me-dia and entertainment have become an on-demand business that regu-larly seeks to redefine what is truth and how we see reality.

The role of the church in the lives of our students is now more important than ever. Generation Z is on the move to find truth. They are looking for mentors. They need older generations to guide them. The good news is that they recognize it. So as culture continues to shift the standard in new and dangerous directions, and before we completely lose sight of truth; the church needs to draw a clear line in the sand about what is true. The church is built on the foundation of Christ as truth, and it is the job of the body of Christ to proclaim that truth with confidence. That means the church will need to stand firm, be different, and be counter-cultural. Because if the church does not offer something different than what the world offers, the church will have nothing to offer.

CONCLUSION

As we engage in conversation with people about their worldview, the notion of truth is at the core. Understanding worldviews direct us in the way people view truth. Do they defend what is true with something they have been told and have little evidence for? Or do they have a well-researched idea of the world, where it came from, the nature of people, and life after death? Do they perceive truth as differing cultural norms to be interpreted by the individual? Asking questions (lots of questions) will help you determine how they see faith, reason and, most of all, truth.

Our job in apologetics is to use questions to help the person see that everyone needs to have good reasons to believe in anything. Then we have the opportunity to show that Christianity has the best reasons for faith in Jesus Christ.

So how do we *know*, or how can we *know*, anything at all? It is our worldview that defines our ability to "know" and, in the same way, what we know provides the framework for what we believe. How we view our existence informs us of how we acquire and process knowledge. For the atheist, the only things that can be known with any certainty are those things discovered and tested through science. Everything else is defined through a subjective lens, each one interpreting reality independent of any objective standard. Consequently, there is very little that can be known with any clear certainty, comfortably leaving much of this world a mystery—things like the origin of the universe and the purpose of humanity.

Conversely, the Christian worldview suggests that through the divine revelation of God in Jesus Christ, we have come to a knowledge of the truth. In other words, because of God, we can know. We can know the origin of the universe, the purpose of humanity, and the reasons for pain in our world and the solution. Christians call this truth. This truth is based on an objective standard known as God—a truth revealed by faith and strengthened by reason. We know Christianity to be true primarily by the self-authenticating witness of God's Spirit. We show Christianity is true by presenting good arguments for its central claims. Therefore to be effective in doing apologetics, we must present rational and persuasive arguments for the gospel in the power of the Holy Spirit and leave the results to God.

CONVERSATION STARTER

Truth is something that is increasingly becoming lost in our world. It seems we are gravitating toward a much more subjective view of things concerning morality, faith, etc.

Take some time and explore some of the everyday statements that we make, that, in reality, contradict or defeat itself. Why is it important that we are careful about how we speak?

DISCOVERING TRUTH

CHAPTER EIGHT
FAITH AND SCIENCE

It was 1996. I was a sophomore at Michigan State University. I was sitting in my dorm room agonizing over my major. Freshman year I had switched from psychology to undeclared and then, as a sophomore, it was time to make a decision. My mom, bless her heart and desire to help, suggested one of the most sought-after careers in the 90's. She convinced me to switch to engineering. Thinking back, I really can't remember why. But after a long conversation, some yelling, and some tears, I found myself making the 30-minute walk to drop off the necessary paperwork.

The next several months were filled with math, science, and CAD classes. All of the subjects I struggled with. As I said, I can't remember why I let her convince me. The tipping point came during junior year. I finally made it through calculus 1 and 2. I made it through chemistry, and I made it through my CAD classes. I didn't do well, but I made it. That was until calculus 3. I tried. I really did. However, despite my best efforts, several all-nighters, my final grade landed on a solid 0.0. I was now absolutely certain of what I already knew: science and math are not my thing.

I so despised the sciences that—to be entirely transparent—as a teacher, I would tell students that if given a choice between theology and science, it would be wise of them to choose theology. A part of me was joking around, but the reality is that I wanted students to focus on Jesus more that math, science, or even technology. As exciting as the world of STEM is for our world in countless ways, I purposed to keep science in a space all its own, distant from Jesus' prominent place in culture. I made science an enemy of the church.

Then, I discovered that there once was a time when theology was considered the queen of the sciences. The pursuit of serving God and the church was society's highest calling. Today, that story is far different. In a world where the church founded public education and institutions of higher learning, the Church has been excommunicated from its cultural roots and its rich heritage. Modern science is now the king of all things education and the study of God reduced to, according to Richard Dawkins, a past time reserved for the delusional.[39] Before the Age of Enlightenment, the beauty of the natural world, although only vaguely understood, was nothing less than a window into the magnificence of God. In the age of Modernity and Postmodernism, man-made natural laws have since reduced creation's beauty and complexity to systems and machinery.

There was a time when belief in God and science enjoyed the perfect romance. Today there stands a seemingly unmovable wedge driven between the two fostering an unprecedented divide and hostility. Some—Christians and non-Christians alike—have offered plenty of opinions about how faith and science ought (or ought not) to exist in the same space and time. Can they get along? Should we just agree to disagree? Can science explain all there is? Or do we need God more than ever? If the Bible is speaking primarily about God's sovereignty and modern science is primarily speaking about natural laws and physical events, is there a conflict at all?

Let's just suppose for a minute that science really can explain all there is. Even if God did get it all started, brilliant minds like Stephen Hawking have suggested that any kind of creator—if one such existed, "has since left the universe to evolve according to them and does not now intervene in it."[40] In other words, science has now taken over where God left off. But you don't need to be a genius like Stephen Hawking to make such an argument for the immense role that science plays and the unnecessary nature of faith. Actor, comedian, singer, and songwriter, Tim Minchin, commented, "Science adjusts its views based on what's observed. Faith is the denial of observation so that belief can be preserved."[41] There is little doubt that modern science has intentionally distanced herself from all things religious. Yet this relationship in tension is nothing new to the modern world.

A HISTORY OF CONFLICT

In his 1875 work, *History of the Conflict Between Religion and Science*, John William Draper, summarizes and reduces the conflict down to simple politics and power. Specifically, the struggle between science and Christianity became apparent when Christianity as a faith, was, as he noted, politicized by Constantine.[42] He argues that Christianity has no credible legs to stand on short of ecclesiastical tradition throughout antiquity. "Roman Christianity and Science are recognized by their respective adherents as being absolutely incompatible; they can-not exist together; one must yield to the other; mankind must make its choice—it cannot have both."[43] It is, of course, this thinking that has seeped into our world's postmodern minds collecting dust in the private sphere of a dualistic worldview.

Instead of denying the credibility of faith, today's Christian accepts the perceived reality that faith and science, the church and the lab, have no business interfering with one another by privatizing one's faith experience and willingly living with an inconsistent and often incoherent worldview. Every day there are well-respected members of the science community that will openly deny the credibility of their faith while "on the job," and yet attend Bible studies, church worship each Sunday, and regularly pray. Faith in Christ is something designed to be kept personal and private, not meant for—or even worthy of—public discourse. Whereas science is then elevated to royalty in the realm of topics to be discussed, debated, honored, or pursued in the public arena.

It would, of course, seem that an atheistic worldview is an appropriate conclusion for the properly and scientifically informed person. After all, if God is nothing more than mindless wishful thinking, removed from scientific inquiry, then what choice do we have but to accept what science has determined a delusion. Therefore making belief in God to be void of any real meaning in life; even if it meant a baseless existence, no life beyond this, and void of any purpose or morality. If science and religion are mutually exclusive; if God is no longer needed to explain the world around us, atheism remains comfortably seated on its throne.

THE MAKING OF A STRAW MAN

Some atheistic scientists often believe it is their calling and purpose in life to be evangelists for their cause. Not only denying the existence—or need for the existence—of god of any kind, but even challenging

Christians to prove the existence of God by way of scientific discovery. But this is precisely where science falls short and begins to dabble in areas that they are neither trained for nor natural science designed for. Atheistic science assumes that Christians understand God to be some kind of object in or part of the created order to be discovered and observed. It is almost as if God is some kind of deity sitting high on a mountain waiting for us to discover him.[44] And if science can't do it, then there is no sense in making such an attempt. Alister McGrath refutes this ridiculous misunderstanding on the part of atheists by reminding us that, "God is not an 'entity' alongside the other entities in the world but rather the source, ground for an explanation of all that exists. God is the creator of all things, not a member of this class of things."[45]

What we are looking at here is a straw man. When atheists (and science) use the word god, they mean something quite different than when I use the name, *God*. In Dawkins famous (or maybe infamous) labeling of God in his book, *The God Delusion*, he is describing several characteristics of God that he assumes are normative. Which results in an entire career spent evangelizing for the denial of such a God. If his view of God were the correct and Christian view of God, I would most certainly join him in his crusade. He—and many others—create their image of God and argue against its existence, and it becomes a polemic against a notion of God that has almost no resemblance of what is taught in Christian theology.[46] McGrath further notes,

> "The atheist critique of Christianity at this point amounts
> to little more than a circular argument concerning the in-

ternal consistencies of atheism, rather than a considered engagement with what Christians believe about God."[47]

If the new atheists and the science they propagate is misrepresenting Christians, theology, and ultimately God, several questions remain unanswered. What role does (or should) science play in the observable world? Where does science fall short and theology step in? Is there any way these two seemingly polar opposite disciplines can each play their role in succinct harmony?

THE ROLE OF SCIENCE

It is what you learned as a kid in grade school—the role and meaning of science. So, to keep science in its proper perspective, let's keep this as simple as possible. From their earliest days in the classroom, children are taught that science provides endless joy in discovery. They learn that doing science is about using the scientific method to uncover mysteries of the observable world—the world that captivates our five senses.

Merriam-Webster defines science as, "knowledge about or study of the natural world based on facts learned through experiments and observation."[48] Notice that according to this definition and what every kid is taught in elementary school, is that science is the study of the natural world and that this study is done through the process of the scientific method—proposing a question, creating a hypothesis, testing the hypothesis, and the analysis of those results. Whether a kid's science fair or major, groundbreaking scientific discoveries, the scientific method helps scientists create credible investigations that feature well-supported evidence. To do so, it must remain religiously neutral. When used as intended, it does not support religious belief nor deny it.[49] So in other words, science is designed for discovery and prepared for any potential result including allowing for God to be apart of the reasoning behind scientific conclusions.

Science is not creating laws of nature, rather it simply discovers them and understands then how to apply those laws. There must be some essential and foundational beliefs about the natural world that science needs to draw from to perform its intended purpose. For example, science cannot determine that the universe is regular, orderly, and rational. It can only discover the truth that the universe is regular, orderly, and rational. Science also must assume that human sense perception and reason are reliable, and the regular patterns of material behavior are intelligible to the human mind. Otherwise, scientists own conclusions would be suspect and untrustworthy. This is precisely why early scientists did not see a chasm between belief in God and science. In fact, the goal of science was to think God's thoughts after him.[50] Faith was not private, nor merely intellectual assent, it was the foundation for the entire scientific enterprise.[51] After all, how else could humanity trust their minds as minds that have knowledge about the world if there is no Godlike rationality hardwired into the image of man?

This is precisely the problem with Darwin and his theory of evolution. If Darwin is right, then our minds have evolved as part of a mindless, unguided process. But if the current state of my mind—the one that just learned it is a product of a mindless, unguided process—is as such, I have no reason to trust it. If this is the way we are supposed to do science, then the whole thing is suspect. John Lennox, professor of mathematics at Oxford, wrote that if atheism is right about science and that God has no business in their business, then it would be much like, "if you knew your computer was the product of a mindless, unguided process, you wouldn't trust it. So to me, atheism undermines the rationality I need to do science."[52] In other words, if atheists are to be intellectually honest, they must admit that they cannot do science if they are coming to the table with the presupposition that God does not exist and try to prove somehow that science disproves religion.

Despite the clear philosophical contradictions, atheists continue to attempt to highjack science as the end all, be all explanation for everything. This, of course, includes matters traditionally belonging to the church, and therefore, furthering the chasm between science and religion. The atheistic scientists continue to assert the doctrine of absolute triumph over religion and only scientific explanation has any validity, according to the atheists.[53] If there is no explanation currently, then you must run with the current version until a better—nonreligious—explanation emerges. But despite the plea of atheists, science has its limits.

TAKE IT TO THE LIMITS

No matter how hard the atheists try, science can only take us so far. Certainly, with the help of science, we can accomplish a lot. Gain a lot of knowledge. Cover a lot of ground. And know a lot about the world around us. Think of the many disciplines of science—so much more than just the natural sciences. Science can influence law, economics, sociology, politics, and psychology. And these, of course, are piled on top of physics, chemistry, and biology. Each of the disciplines serves a small part of the larger whole.

Imagine for a moment, your last birthday cake—but with a piece missing. Your mom places the cake in front of you, candles burning, people warming up to sing, and there it sits, one big slice of cake missing. It is an incomplete cake. Instead of enjoying your cake and the singing, you can't help but wonder, "Who took that slice?" The same holds true of the totality of science. Each scientific discipline is only one slice of the cake. Some slices are larger than others. Each has its limits in explanatory power and scope, but each plays a vital role. Ideally, each compliments, rather than contradicts each other.

But we have left out one important piece of the cake— theological analysis and discovery. Despite what atheists would have us believe, theology is a piece and religion is the lens by which we see the rest of the disciplines. For example, McGrath notes, "the Christian will speak of God bringing the world into existence and direction it toward its intended outcomes. For some, this process involves direct divine action; for others, it involves God creating and working through natural forces to achieve those goals."[54]

Science can only take us so far, and there are only so many questions it can answer. Science can discover new truths about nature, but it cannot answer the ultimate question of why we have something in nature rather than nothing, or what makes humanity so significant above all other creatures in nature. But if we see scientific discipline through the lens of God as Creator, we see how God reveals Himself in nature, and we see order and design as part of that creation. Science cannot claim to prove that miracles never happen, nor can it prove that a miracle did happen. Science can only explain that a particular event operated inconsistently with how we understand natural laws. The claim that science disproves miracles is not a scientific claim, but a philosophical or religious claim.

ISN'T THE BIBLE ENOUGH?

But I would also argue that the same holds true for religious claims. Christians, often in an attempt to bridge the gap between science and religion, look to the highest authority, the Bible as the final answer. The expectation here is to look solely to the Bible for scientific guidance. Nowhere is this more prevalent than inside the discussion of the age of the earth and theistic evolution. Thoughts, feelings, theories, and conclusions are as numerous as many other theological disagreements and differences within Christendom, maybe more so.

Both of these topics revolve around the larger issue of Christian theology's historical parents, Adam and Eve. Did God directly create these two as the Bible describes or is the earliest story in Genesis some kind of metaphorical parable or poem? This question is, of course, answered differently depending on where one stands along the theological spectrum and the role one expects science and the Bible to play. On one end is what is known as special creationists. The belief here is simply a literal six-day creation, a literal Adam and Eve, and the Genesis account of creation to be unquestionable. On the other end is what is commonly known as theistic evolution, which attempts to describe evolution as the instrument God used to create life and that Adam and Eve are nothing more than poetic symbols. Hovering in the middle is what is called progressive creationists.[55] This perspective works to take into consideration evidence for an older earth without compromising the integrity of the Bible. But is there a right view? And if so, which is it?

I do not have the room here for such a deep exposition, but allow me to make some brief comments as it relates to our discussion about the relationship between faith and science. There are at least two key ideas we must keep in mind when considering the importance of both faith and science. First, we must note that many creationists want to—and for a good reason—make the Bible the sole authority for all things including science. This means of course that Genesis chapters 1-11 must be the primary text for our scientific knowledge of how the universe came to be. However, the problem with this is that Genesis 1-11 is not a science book, nor was it ever intended to give us a scientific account of human origins. Rather, "it is a creation story to be understood by all peoples, be they ancient or modern, that God is the Father of the entire human race."[56]

Second, Genesis is about establishing a biblical worldview—including that of creation—not refuting Darwin's theory of evolution. Genesis provides the necessary context in which we see and understand the rest of the biblical narrative and God's redemptive story. We cannot understand salvation without understanding the need for salvation. We cannot understand our need for salvation without seeing the effects of sin. We cannot see the effects of sin without seeing the beauty, majesty, and sovereignty of God's creation; all of which we get a glimpse of in the early stages of Genesis. New Testament theologian and professor, Michael Bird, suggests that,

> "[The creation account in Genesis], is a theologically embedded story of God's creation of the human race; a story with characters as real as the earth they stand on, and yet

they stand for more than being our primal parents, as their story testifies to the creative power of God over the world of human beings and explains how God's perfect paradise went wrong."[57]

Approaching science with a biblical worldview means allowing science to fill out areas or offer suggestions where the Bible is not designed to speak on, but to do so without contradicting the authority of the biblical text, or changing our interpretation to fit a particular scientific theory. Approaching science with a biblical worldview means approaching science with the very mind of God.

CONCLUSION

The church must not shy away from the power and beauty of scientific discovery. But the church must also engage in it critically. The scientific method, when applied properly does not need to be an enemy of faith. However, we run into problems when we assume that science can answer (or at least provide the credible attempt) to every question. Science has its limits. Science is limited to the physical world, whereas faith deals the metaphysical and physical. Christians cannot allow atheists to smuggle in their presuppositions and claim intellectual superiority. Christians can equally engage in robust intellectual discussions and contributions—and do so from a greater vantage point—of the historical origins and the explanatory successes of the natural sciences.[58] For the Christian, science can offer an incredible gateway to God's created order. Although not technically a scientist, King David may have said it best.

"The heavens declare the glory of God; the sky displays his handiwork. Day after day it speaks out; night after night it reveals his greatness. There is no actual speech or word, nor is its voice literally heard. Yet its voice echoes throughout the earth; its words carry to the distant horizon. In the sky he has pitched a tent for the sun." Psalm 19:1-4

If science is the discovery of the natural world that we can observe, then for the Christian, science is the discovery of God's created order. The more we know, the more we come to know the mind of God, the mysteries, the beauty, the complexity, the simplicity, the order, and intricate design of all that is. Science, when properly used, is the gateway to discovering the glory of God.[59]

CONVERSATION STARTER

Faith and science are not opposites, enemies, or even frienemies. Instead, science has the potential to give us greater faith. Ask your students to explore how they might look for evidence of God in the secular science books they use in school every day.

How can you deal with the objections science raise in regards to religion?

CHAPTER NINE
THE REALITY OF THE CREATOR

Imagine a world without a concept of God. Imagine a world without even the slightest idea of God or a god, deity, higher power, creator, or anything remotely similar. Imagine a world where God is dead. The famous philosopher and atheist Friedrich Nietzsche imagined such a world proclaiming that "God is dead...and we have killed him."

> "God is dead. God remains dead. And we have killed him. How shall we comfort ourselves, the murderers of all murderers? What was holiest and mightiest of all that the world has yet owned has bled to death under our knives: who will wipe this blood off us? What water is there for us to clean ourselves? What festivals of atonement, what sacred games shall we have to invent? Is not the greatness of this deed too great for us? Must we not become gods simply to appear worthy of it?"[60]

Nietzsche was speaking of a world that no longer saw the reality of God as relevant—a world in the midst of the Enlightenment educating themselves past the need for God. But what would it mean? What would the death of God mean for humanity, how we see the physical world, and how we see morality? Even Nietzsche, a pastor's son turned atheist, understood the incredibly dangerous implications of a godless world.

Now in the twenty-first century, this view continues to persistently push its way to center stage. Although there is not one view of God or even of reality, which seems to dominate the melting pot of western culture, postmodern thought continues to challenge the relevancy of God in the modern world.

If modern thought brought us the enlightenment, scientific discovery, and driving out the need for God, then postmodern stands in square contrast to the conventional and conformity of the 19th century. Postmodernism, stemming from relativism, views truth as relative and therefore our views on God and his relevancy to modern culture relative as well. We have, therefore, moved beyond definition, distinction, and objective standards to allowing personal, subjective preference to create a kind of truth that has become whatever it needs to mean to you, and the rest of us have no right or reason to question it. So if Nietzsche claimed that God is dead, then postmodern's claim is that God might be dead, if that works for you. Or he can be alive if that works for you. In fact, God can even be your purple-spotted half monkey, and half rabbit that you imagine is your friend if that works for you.

The world we engage in is one of confusion, self-preservation and of relative moral values. The scary reality of this is that a person could be open to hearing your view, accepting your view, liking your view and even go so far as to agree with you in many instances, yet still hold that your view is just that, *your* view. This is what happens when people refuse to recognize and accept absolute truth. Everything is up for grabs: morals, definitions of words and what we consider truth. In other words, postmodern thinkers claim that objective truth has given way to personal taste, or a subjective reality in every area of life, claiming with absolute certainty of the absence of absolute truth. So in this chapter, we will explore the lens through which people view reality: one based entirely on experience and an external, objective standard. From there we will discuss what it looks like to build a comprehensive and convincing case for Christian theism.

WHAT IS REAL?

As children of God, we view reality through the story that God is telling through Scripture. But what about those who do not see the world through the same lens as Christians? Is their reality somehow different? Could it be possible that just because I view reality in one particular way, someone else could view reality in another way? And if so, how can that be if absolute truth prevails over the self-defeating nature of relativism? If realities can be different, then certainly truth can change as well. However, since we have already determined truth must be constant and absolute, then we need to understand the nature of reality and discover how we can define it.

As Christians, we view the world through a lens that assumes the existence of God. It is impossible to view it otherwise. But what about those who have a different view of a god or do not believe in a god at all? How can reality be described and defined? We know that God exists by the revelation of the Spirit, but how do you introduce the idea and existence of God to someone who has never experienced the Spirit—let alone believe in him—nor sees the world as you do because they have a different view of reality?

The postmodern view argues that it is perfectly justified to create one's reality based on such experience; each person's unique experience, therefore, leads to his or her unique reality. So it becomes a question of what is real. Neo's perception of reality is instantly changed by his experience with one simple pill in the 1999 film, *The Matrix*. The movie, *The Hitchhiker's Guide to the Galaxy* illustrates existential reality perfectly. In one scene, a whale suddenly comes into existence out of nothing. Beyond the absurdity of such an event, the whale begins to reconcile his existence with his experience, discovering himself and the sensation of falling to the earth. While he plummets to certain death, the whale begins to name things and his experience with them. As the whale describes the world around him, and himself, he sees a large round like object coming at him very quickly. He names this object "ground" and briefly—before meeting the ground face to face with incredible velocity—wonders if it will be his friend.

Although a bit ridiculous, this scene holds incredible truth for the way many come to grips with reality. A reality based entirely on specific personal experience. However, no matter how much the whale desires the ground to be his friend, no matter how exciting it can be to feel the wind, the reality is he is going to die upon impact. Despite the whale's perceived reality, the absolute truth of reality will reveal its dire consequences. In the same way, no matter how we wish to look at or define reality to suit our experience and our needs, there are always consequences for getting it wrong.

This scenario describes just one version of reality—one of many views of reality that are quite varied and numerous. However, to help us better understand them, we will narrow them into four basic ideas.

Reality is just an illusion–Have you ever had a dream you were sure was real or had the eerie thought that maybe although you think you are awake, you might be dreaming right now? In the movie, *The Matrix*, once again, the question asked is: what is real? All that Neo (the main character, played by Keanu Reaves) knew was just a dream; only a reality in his mind, but not the "really real." So according to this view, no matter what we think we see and experience, reality could exist behind the visual perception, almost as if there is a veil put over our eyes to mask what is real. Hollywood plays with this kind of scenario quite frequently. Think of more recent movies like *Inception* or *Doctor Strange*. Both of these films suggest a reality that goes far beyond what we think we see.

The world was self-created–According to this view, the universe was created by chance through a series of random circumstances, essentially creating itself over an undetermined period, all on its own. In other words, the universe and reality as we know it, just popped into existence. Realistically, this is logically impossible. Everything you see, all that is around you, logically must come from something or someone. If I plan to play a game of football with some friends, I make sure we have a ball (along with anything else we need). It would be absurd to arrive at a field without a ball fully expecting one to just pop into existence. If you were to start with nothing, then nothing will come. Except for God himself (which we will take on later), it is logically impossible for something to come from nothing.

The universe is self-existent–Instead of giving the universe an arbitrary starting point, a self-existent universe is one that has always been there. Somehow, the universe is eternal. Have you ever considered the idea of infinity? Now think of a universe with no beginning and no end. In all those fancy math classes I took in college, I learned that infinity is only a concept that logically comes to a mathematical contradiction. No matter how large the number or what function you try with infinity, you are still never any closer to infinity than when you began. Further, something that exists inside a measure of time cannot be infinite. Something finite has a clear beginning and ending point. But infinity has no end and no beginning. So, if I am trying to measure a fixed point in time—for example, my birthday—then how do I measure a fixed point within a construct that has no fixed points? In other words, if there was an infinite series of moments leading up to the moment of my birthday, but infinity has no beginning and no end, then how did I get to the moment of my birthday? This is illogical.

Created–Something or someone outside the elements and confines of time created the universe. We cannot suppose that everything around us is eternal. How is it possible that a living plant that grows and dies could repeat such a process eternally? We also cannot suppose that the universe just popped into being. Think of the impossibility of an object simply popping into existence in front of you as you walked down the street. If an object cannot come from nowhere, then how could the universe? Finally, we cannot suppose all that we see around us is just an illusion. Therefore the best-case scenario is that the universe was created. However, to be clear, this does not prove or assume the existence of a monotheistic Christian idea of God. It does, however, illustrate the necessity and logical conclusion for a created universe.

ALTERNATIVE REALITIES

Reality is the foundation for a person's worldview. It guides our understanding and forms our opinions. Just like Nietzsche, the death of God is the starting point for postmodern thinking; essentially what we call a presupposition. In other words, a presupposition is a foundational idea that informs all other ideas. The reality that defines postmodernism lacks a clear definition of a physical reality. Postmodernism does not address a concrete reality but instead addresses how language constructs meaning. For example, instead of the reality of the universe beginning through a series of cataclysmic events known as the Big Bang, postmodernism would instead search for what was meant by the universe. If reality is where one begins, postmodernism begins with meaning.

Conversely, Pantheism, including the traditional beliefs of Hindus, finds reality within Brahman, the essence of the whole Soul of the cosmos. "The phenomenal world of matter and of individualized consciousness—the world of things and animals and men and even gods—is the manifestation of a Divine Ground within which all partial realities have their being, and apart from which they would be nonexistent."[61] To simplify this, we could say that the Divine Ground, also known as Brahman, is the soul, or source for all existence. This makes every piece of creation a piece of the Divine Ground. Everything that exists is god. Otherwise, it is an illusion or nonexistent. Reality does not come from separate distinctions of, for example, objects like chairs, people, or cars. Instead, reality arises out of oneness of the Divine Ground or Brahman. "To know reality is to pass beyond distinction, to 'realize' the oneness of all by being one with all."[62] In other words, to know reality is to become one with the Divine Ground.

Without the existence of God or a Divine Ground to explain the nature of reality, for the atheist, science and the natural world must fill that role. For the Theist, reality is buried in a personal Creator of all that is. For the Deist, God may remain existent, but loses His personality, and therefore reality is once again altered. But for the atheist, God is reduced to an annoyance getting in the way of true scientific discovery. Reality can only be discovered through what science can tell us about the natural world. With God out of the picture, the cosmos becomes the center of attention.

When Nietzsche wrote, "God is dead," he certainly understood the incredible importance of defining reality.

"Whither is God?" he cried; "I will tell you. We have killed him -- you and I. All of us are his murderers. But how did we do this? How could we drink up the sea? Who gave us the sponge to wipe away the entire horizon? What were we doing when we unchained this earth from its sun? Whither is it moving now? Whither are we moving? Away from all suns? Are we not plunging continually? Backward, sideward, forward, in all directions? Is there still any up or down? Are we not straying, as through an infinite nothing? Do we not feel the breath of empty space? Has it not become colder? Is not night continually closing in on us? Do we not need to light lanterns in the morning? Do we hear nothing as yet of the noise of the gravediggers who are burying God? Do we smell nothing as yet of the divine decomposition? Gods, too, decompose. God is dead. God remains dead. And we have killed him.[63]

Nietzsche recognized that the means by which the world was explained—the way in which people saw reality—would need to be completely reinvented. Everything must be changed and redefined. But if we know for certain that experience does not shape reality, and instead of reality survives independently of anything we do, think or feel, then we can at minimum determine that objective reality must exist. The whale in *The Hitchhikers Guide To The Galaxy*, as it fell to the ground, could think anything he wanted about every part of his experience, and yet in reality, within a few moments, he would be dead. Further, we could conclude that the whale could have created meaning through a divine origin, felt a sense of oneness, or even felt a sense of moral obligation to befriend the approaching earth. But does anything of these ideologies express objective reality or truth?

While it is safe to assume that our experiences play a part in shaping one's worldview, it is possible a person's worldview could be mistaken. Reality is not something subjective or dependent upon human interpretation. Reality is objective and independent from human interaction (or in our example, whale interaction). But what about reality based on scientific discovery, or that god is a part of everything? How can one know if those realities are false, and the reality of Christian theism true?

Knowing what people consider to be "reality" is incredibly helpful when beginning a discussion surrounding the existence of God. Some may rightly assume the existence of some kind of Creator but lack an understanding of the personal aspect of God. Others may see themselves as a god. Still, others may be on Nietzsche's bandwagon. However a person chooses to define reality, we as Christians should be able to point to the concept of knowing absolute truth by knowing Jesus Christ, and therefore knowing the objective truth of reality.

But if the answers to the questions of reality prove to be false in other worldviews, how can Christian Theism be much different? Could it be that the true nature of objective reality has yet to be discovered? To be honest, if there were a clear answer or method of showing that Christian Theism was the absolute correct worldview, then there would be little need for apologetics. So then how can Christians claim that there is a monotheistic, triune God who can be known intimately? How can Christians claim the divinity of Jesus, the inerrancy of Scripture, the moral code written throughout the Bible, or a life beyond the grave?

EVIDENCE OR PROOF?

With every worldview, a person must have some reason for believing what he believes. Even if someone's worldview claims reality is an illusion, he must have a reason for this claim. We could even go as far as to say someone with psychosis, losing all sense of external reality, still retains reasons for what and how he thinks, even if it makes little to no sense.

Despite the need to have reason, we cannot prove beyond the shadow of a doubt that Christian Theism is the correct worldview. However, we can illustrate convincing evidence. In fact, we can provide the best-case scenario, or the best answers to the fundamental questions about reality, humanity and life after death. The goal in every conversation is not to shove the Christian worldview down another person's throat or toss it in front of a person alongside hundreds of other options. The goal is to answer the questions that perplex the other person with the Christian worldview because it answers his question better than any other worldview.

Our evidence is always objective—we can only present the case. As the old saying goes, we can lead a horse to water, but cannot make it drink. No matter how hard we try, evidence for the mind is never persuasion of the will. We can only show the evidence as the collection of facts pointing in the direction of what is true. We never want to say, "I'm going to prove to you God exists." Then you are assuming that the evidence has established the absolute fact, beyond all doubt that God exists. You will sound arrogant, and, chances are, the person you are speaking to will never listen. Not to mention the entire purpose of apologetics is rendered moot.

So then, what qualifies as evidence? It is just a simple matter of cause and effect. If there is a house, then we can suppose that someone built the house. We can say for sure that the house did not spontaneously occur from nothing and that there is an intended design and purpose for the house. So when we are talking about the existence of God, the most simplistic of evidence is the effect. There is something here, as opposed to nothing. We have earth, people and animals, plants, an eco-system and air to breathe in a careful balance. When we talk about God, some of the most striking evidence is the very world we live in and the complexity of creation, from science to philosophy, and from love to war. We have the evidence; our job then is to allow the evidence to point to the cause. Therefore we need to gather as much evidence as possible to present the best possible case. We call this a cumulative case.

CUMULATIVE CASE APPROACH

Because there is no silver bullet argument, it should be always your goal to present the best evidence that delivers the best explanation for reality. We need to gather as much evidence as possible by compiling a cumulative case. To do this, we need to make sure it satisfies the following requirements.[64]

Explanatory Power

The best explanation accounts for all the facts that an alternative and faulty explanation does, but also explains the causes of other facts, which the second one does not take into consideration or cannot account for. In other words, it covers all the necessary facts, true and false, for all differing views; for example, the explanation for the Christian's correct assertion that God exists as well as the explanation for the error of atheistic philosophy.

Explanatory Scope

This covers all the relevant data. It may leave out some but takes in the majority of the data (morality, human knowledge, etc.) necessary for the argument. If explanatory power focuses on the depth of the argument, then explanatory scope focuses on the breadth of the evidence.

Empirical Adequacy

We have observable evidence of the world. In other words, the world we live in is something we can experience. Further, if you have an experience with something, it probably exists, unless you are the in *The Matrix*. Even in the world of apologetics, our experience with God matters.

Rational Consistency

The primary tenets must be logically consistent with one another. There are no contradictions; your view is logical and makes sense as an explanation for the way things are.

Simplicity

It may be possible, but is it plausible? For example, it is possible I could survive a one-on-one fight with a grizzly bear; however, this is not plausible. It may come as a bit of a surprise, but generally speaking, the best answer is often the simplest.

Experiential Relevance

You cannot argue a point of view or a reality that you have not experienced yourself. You could study brain surgery for several years and know everything there is to know about it, yet it would be ridiculous to teach another person how to perform brain surgery if you have never actually operated, regardless of how much you know about it. The same goes for arguing for Christianity. How can you teach or discuss God if you have never experienced Him yourself?

OUR APPROACH TO THE EVIDENCE

The number of objections against a belief in God, let alone Christianity, is countless. Some objections are superficial and uninformed. Others have deep-rooted, negative emotions against anything remotely religious. Still, further, there are many common catch phrases people use to describe their doubt, lack of belief, etc.

One objection is that God is a psychological crutch—help through life in ways you cannot help yourself. Another is the claim that we have no proof that God is there. To some, experience is not sufficient evidence for God. Finally, is the concern for others' experiences of a god. Why should only one experience of God or a god count? These are all legitimate reasons to reject God, and we must deal with each of these (and many more) with care, concern, love, and respect. No person's worldview is dumb or stupid. In fact, just the opposite is true. Worldviews are sacred. All the more reason, we need to find common ground with the person and help him conclude that the worldview he holds is not logically consistent with reality.

Where do we start? How does a conversation begin? How do you meet a person where he is and establish common ground and do so in truth with love? Some people are naturally gifted in beginning conversations, and others are not. Therefore some may pick these principles up quicker than others. However, the important thing is to practice. Like all things worth doing, it requires practice.

As we move through this book, we will build a cumulative case for the truth claims of Christianity. We will begin with the beginning of creation and end with the resurrection of Jesus. Keep in mind we are constructing a total approach. Depending on who you are talking to, you may not need to address every argument every time. Depending on the time you have and the circumstances, you may only be able to tackle one small piece of one argument.

Our approach will be as follows:
The existence of God and the creation of the universe.

The problem of evil and pain.

The reliability of the New Testament Scriptures.

The claims of Jesus Christ.

The resurrection of Jesus Christ.

As we pursue each of these topics, not only will you have the ability and confidence to engage others in conversation about Christianity, but your faith in Christ will gain confidence and strength as well.

CONCLUSION

The nature of reality is tricky because it sits on a presuppositional level. It operates under the surface and informs the rest of a person's belief system. Sometimes it even begs the question (or circular reasoning). The worldview is created from a person's perception of reality, but their reality makes sense to them because of their worldview. Getting people to see through a new set of lenses can only be the work of the Holy Spirit.

CONVERSATION STARTER

God has given us everything we need to be sure that He exists. Although some may claim that what we do have for evidence is not enough.

What would it take? How much evidence would be enough to either believe or solidify your current belief in God?

CHAPTER TEN

MAKING THE CASE FOR A CREATOR

If you have ever sat out at night, far away from the city, and looked up into the night sky, there is no doubt you began to feel very small. You realize the magnitude of the universe and might even begin to ask, who or what else is out there. The greater the technology we create, the farther into space we can see. The farther into space we see, the bigger the universe becomes and, consequently, the smaller we begin to feel. Just how big is the universe? You can't help but wonder what else is out there that we haven't seen.

The book of Genesis tells us that God created the entire universe. This means God created everything we see with the naked eye, everything we can see with the technology we have created, and all the things we have yet to see. If God did create all there is, then why us? Why here? Why is there something here rather than nothing? Can we even know with any certainty that there is a God somewhere, everywhere or elsewhere? What would it all mean if God did not exist?

The existence of God is only a starting point for so many more questions, rather than an ending point with absolute certainty. However, if there is absolute truth and it is something we can know, then that truth must have a starting point, an objective foundation in which we can begin to shape our worldview. Any discussion regarding the nature of the universe must begin with God. There is no use talking to an atheist about the beauty of Jesus, the cross or the resurrection until we have established a clear case for the existence of some sort of Creator. If truth describes the way things are in the world, then Christians must claim that the basis for truth hinges on the existence of God. Therefore, we need to formulate a clear case for the existence of a personal Creator of the universe known as God so that we can establish a sound starting point for faith in Christ.

IN THE BEGINNING, GOD...

Wherever you are sitting, look around you. What do you see? No matter where you are, there is something all around you. Why isn't there nothing? What in the world would that look like? As Christians, we very logically assume that the answer is found in God Himself. We have stuff because He decided to make it. But how in the world do you argue that God is the beginning cause of all things, the only one who could have designed the universe, and the standard for morality?

We can assert three principal cause and effect pieces of evidence that show it is more reasonable to say that God exists, rather than the alternative view that God does not exist. These can get a little complicated, so I prefer to keep things profoundly simple for students (and frankly most of us too) to grab hold of. Over the last ten years, I have used an acronym created by Dr. Norman Geisler to help illustrate this and make it easy to remember—the acronym B-I-G.[65] For each of the arguments for God, we will look at simple, three-point, logical arguments. These are not comprehensive but are meant to create a launch pad for further discussion by laying out the basic principles.

B-UNIVERSE THAT BEGAN REQUIRES A BEGINNER (COSMOLOGICAL ARGUMENT – AS IN THE COSMOS, THE UNIVERSE).

"since what may be known about God is plain to them, because God has made it plain to them. For since the creation of the world God's invisible qualities—his eternal power and divine nature—have been clearly seen, being understood from what has been made, so that people are without excuse." - Romans 1:19-20

"But when the apostles Barnabas and Paul heard of this, they tore their clothes and rushed out into the crowd, shouting: "Friends, why are you doing this? We too are only human, like you. We are bringing you good news, telling you to turn from these worthless things to the living God, who made the heavens and the earth and the sea and everything in them." - Acts 14:14-15

"Paul then stood up in the meeting of the Areopagus and said: "People of Athens! I see that in every way you are very religious. For as I walked around and looked carefully at your objects of worship, I even found an altar with this inscription: to an unknown god. So you are ignorant of the very thing you worship—and this is what I am going to proclaim to you. The God who made the world and everything in it is the Lord of heaven and earth and does not live in temples built by human hands." - Acts 17:22-24

For the everyday Christian, these verses, as well as several others, are enough evidence to illustrate the existence of God and His creation of the universe. Game over right? Well, maybe not. With someone of a different worldview, these verses are no more relevant than the opinion of the average person. So, we need to approach God's existence from a different angle. For our study, at several points, we will set Scripture aside and look for evidence of Christianity beyond the confines of the Bible. I am not trying to demean or disrespect the inspired Word of God, but if the entire universe and everything in it belongs to God, certainly we can find evidence in many places other than the pages of Scripture. This can be incredibly useful when talking to a person who does not accept what the Bible says or has never read it.

Remember, something cannot come from nothing. If the universe began with nothing, then the universe would cease to exist. In other words, if all you have is nothing, then nothing is all you will ever have (or not have—because it is nothing). Se we are claiming that the universe must have a cause or beginning because clearly, the universe exists. So let's take a look to see how this argument works out.

Premise 1: Everything that begins to exist has a cause[66] (see the Law of Causality, one of the fundamental principles of science, which states that everything that comes to be needs a cause). Unless this entire world is an illusion, we clearly have a physical world around us. In other words, something is here. Therefore, logically it must have had a cause, because if we have only nothing, then we will continue to have nothing. Out of nothing, nothing comes.

Go back to that image you had of nothing. Not just a room with no furniture or wall coverings, or even an empty space of some kind. Even an empty space has something: air and the particles that make up the air. The absence of everything is even the absence of space and time. If something could indeed come from nothing, then why don't random objects like "bicycles and Beethoven, and root beer just pop into being from nothing? Why is it only universes that can come into being from nothing?"[67] It seems as though the atheist is picking and choosing which parts of the universe can suddenly come from nothing. What is true of these random objects must be true of the universe in which these objects exist. If there is nothing, there are no properties, nothing to even label as nothing. So logically, to claim that something can come from utter nothingness is absurd.

Premise 2: The universe had a beginning (even the Big Bang Theory suggests this). Whether you choose to stick to the literal biblical creation story or even some sort of or version of the Big Bang Theory, the assertion is still a beginning. But even if the universe couldn't come out of nothing, then couldn't it be argued that the universe has existed infinitely? As we previously discussed, if it was indeed possible for the universe to be infinite there must have been an infinite number of past events leading up to the event of me typing this page and you reading it. Sounds easy enough, right?

The problem here is how we deal with infinity. Most of us when we are working with infinity are working with it in a theoretical or potential way. In other words, we use the idea of infinity to describe a limit in math that is never reached. I could potentially count in sequence, 1, 2, 3,...and so on to infinity. But I will never actually reach it. Therein lies the problem. If we are talking about the universe, we must deal with infinity in an actual way. If I thought of an infinite universe the same way I thought of numbers, then I would be counting backward with no actual destination. If I have no destination, then how did I arrive where I am at this moment? Where on the scale between 0 and infinity are we right at this moment? It is impossible to count to infinity because no matter how many numbers I count to; there will always be an infinite number of numbers left to count. The same holds true for going backward. Therefore, you cannot experience an infinite number of finite moments. The only conclusion left is that since the universe is comprised of a series of finite moments in time, the universe must have had a beginning.

Conclusion: Therefore the universe had a cause. Since everything that exists had a beginning and every beginning requires a cause, the universe must have a cause. Christians, of course, call this cause God, but this argument does not necessarily prove the existence of God. It does, however, offer sound logic and a practical conclusion for a cause of the universe. Notice the logical progression of thought. Simple, easy to remember and each point offers more to expand on if needed. However, no argument is free from objections.

Possible objections

First, who made God? The easy answer is nobody. He is eternal and does not need a cause. Is this too easy? If everything needs a cause, then the only way to explain the universe is to suggest an uncaused causer. The most common objection is this simple question of God's origin. If we are insistent on explaining the origin of the universe, then shouldn't we be equally insistent to explain the origin of God? However, imagine if we were to have an answer for the origin of God. Would He remain God? Or would the thing that caused God, be considered God? When we speak of God, we mean the means by which all things came into being. We call this an uncaused causer. To ask the question of God's origin is known as a category mistake. The questions do not pertain to the nature of God. It would be like asking, "what does the color blue taste like?" The category of taste does not belong to the color blue. Thus the question is absurd. The same holds true for "who made God?" The category of origin does not belong to God. Otherwise, He would cease to be what we know as God. His character is dependent on being uncaused. Further, things that follow the Law of Causality are only those within the restraints of time. God is outside time, and created time, thereby incarnating Himself within time in the man Jesus Christ.

Second, even if the universe had a cause, why does the cause have to be what you call God? If we address this objection ontologically, we can argue that what we call "God" is the highest or greatest possible existence that humans can imagine or conceive of. So in the case of what causes the universe, if it is anything less than God, there must be something greater that caused it. Therefore we would call that God.

I - THE UNIVERSE IS INTELLIGENTLY DESIGNED (THIS IS ALSO KNOWN AS THE TELEOLOGICAL ARGUMENT)

The heavens declare the glory of God;
the skies proclaim the work of his hands.

Day after day they pour forth speech;
night after night they reveal knowledge.

They have no speech, they use no words;
  no sound is heard from them.

Yet their voice goes out into all the earth,
  their words to the ends of the world.
In the heavens God has pitched a tent for the sun.

  It is like a bridegroom coming out of his chamber,
  like a champion rejoicing to run his course.

It rises at one end of the heavens
  and makes its circuit to the other;
  nothing is deprived of its warmth. - Psalm 19:1-6

Without anything close to the scientific knowledge we have today, David could look into the sky and see the incredible design of God's creation. He knew that God had done something incredible within the scope of creation and that each day was a divine gift.

Premise 1: If you were to take a stroll on a trail through a dense forest—seemingly in the middle of nowhere. You have no cell service, no roads—nothing but forest. Along the trail, you see a rock formation that spells "help." As you look at this odd and seemingly rare formation, you easily conclude that this is a result of animals, or erosion, or some other natural random event that caused this formation of rocks. Of course, you wouldn't conclude that! There is no doubt that you would assume that another person in the forest now or sometime in the past needed help and used the rocks to spell out the word. It was designed.

Every design has a designer. Think in concrete terms, like a chair, a desk, or a computer. These things do not design themselves as some random ordering of products. You could even go as far as to compare the design of the universe to a well-designed building or bridge. Any measurement that is off could cause the bridge to fail or the building to crumble. The same holds true for the highly complex universe.

Premise 2: The universe has a highly complex design. Most of us take for granted the intricacy of our bodies. An eyeball and its incredible complexity and ability to process light, interpret images and process them in the brain. A single DNA molecule, the building block of all life, carries the same amount of information as one volume of an encyclopedia. No one seeing an encyclopedia lying in the forest would hesitate to think that it had an intelligent cause, so if we find a living creature composed of millions of DNA-based cells, we ought to assume that, likewise, it has an intelligent cause. Michael Behe, the author of *Darwin's Black Box*, rightly concludes, "The result of these cumulative efforts to investigate the cell—to investigate life at the molecular level—is a loud, clear, piercing cry of 'design!'"[68]

Conclusion: Therefore, since the universe is clearly designed and all design requires a designer, the universe had a designer. This line of argument is great for the scientific mind, and I only scratched the surface. It seems that the more complexity we discover in the universe, the more it reveals the nature of design and an intellect mind behind it all. As we noted earlier, science is not something Christians need to fear or shy away from. Whether or not science is something that some easy to you, there are excellent resources that not only make it easier to understand but also exciting to discover.

Potential Objections:

Couldn't complexity explain evolution? Every day that you walk outside, the blueprint for design is all around you whether you realize it or not. Oxygen levels in the atmosphere are so balanced that one minor adjustment too high or too low, plants and animals would cease to exist. If the earth's magnetic field were stronger, then electromagnetic storms would be too severe for us to survive. If our distance from the moon were any different, the effects on the atmosphere would be cataclysmic. Any change in the earth's tilt and the temperature of the earth's surface rises too high, and we burn up. The earth is positioned just right within the galaxy and just the right distance from the sun— too far away, we freeze, to close, we fry. These are just a spattering of the evidence of how the earth has been fine-tuned so that life can exist on the planet. One slight alteration and life could not survive.

G-Moral Law Requires a Giver of this Moral Law.

The moral law deals with what is good versus what is evil. Every law that says we should do good and not evil has a lawgiver. This tends to be one of the most discussed topics because it relates to man on a deeply personal level. The argument is as follows:

Premise 1: Every law has a lawgiver. This goes back to the argument of something from nothing. If there is a law, someone had to come up with it. For those who believe in God, this is very simple: God serves as the basis or origin for morality. But what about the atheist? If God does not exist, where do morals come from? If humans are considered nothing more than higher functioning animals, then we should be held to the same moral standard as any other animal: survival, instinct, reproduction, etc. So morals would not exist. There would be no murder, no rape, no theft, or any other kind of evil one could imagine. Further, if rape, for example, were not wrong, then a woman would not be justified in feeling, "wronged" when such a violent crime is committed against her. Where does the impact of being wronged originate from and why do bystanders feel a sense of moral obligation to see the perpetrator suffer the appropriate punishment?

Premise 2: There is a moral law. We certainly have morals. Most (if not all) would agree that it is wrong to take the life of another without just cause. Every society holds people accountable for such actions. However, the question remains, how can we determine such levels of morality? Consider the concepts of fairness, values, accountability, and guilt. Can you think of any place or any time when it would be acceptable to rape a woman or abuse a child? Even the very thought of such a crime makes us cringe. Why? Because there is an objective moral law.

Conclusion: Therefore, there is a moral lawgiver. Many, instead, will try to assert the presence of relative moral laws. In this case, social systems are responsible for creating moral standards instead of one unified source or standard. At first glance, this seems to make sense. There are many customs and practices considered part of the social norm in one culture while in another considered obscene. Even in the United States, there is great debate surrounding the morality of things like same-sex marriage and issues of sexual identity. But having a difference of opinion on moral values does not preclude a universal moral standard with subjectivism that can change whenever the culture decides.

So we have a question of who is the moral hero. If we were to jump on the skeptic's bandwagon and proclaim that we have no use for God when deciding what we consider moral or immoral, we only have a couple of options to consider. Morality is either a human invention crafted over time and based on accepted evolutionary principles, or morality is an eternal construct etched into the fabric of the universe—something that has always been.

First, let's consider humanity as its own moral standard. According to philosopher, neuroscientist, and author, Sam Harris, the more we know about the brain, the more we can understand humanity's pursuit of a higher morality. In his book, *The Moral Landscape*, Harris argues that any moral understanding or achievement produced from religion has occurred only by accident. For Harris, "meaning, values, morality, and the good life must relate to facts about the well-being of conscious creatures—and, in our case, must lawfully depend upon events in the world and upon states of the human brain."[69] Humanity is therefore responsible for moral development and advancement. The more we know, the more moral we can become. At least that is the idea. Philosopher, Peter Singer echoes this same view.

"The core of ethics runs deep in our species and is common to human beings everywhere. It survives the most appalling hardships and the most ruthless attempts to deprive human beings of their humanity. Nevertheless, some people resist the idea that his core has a biological basis which we have inherited from our pre-human ancestors."[70]

However good this perspective may sound on the surface, Harris, Singer, and many others like them forget some basic principles of logic. Allowing humanity to stand in the place of its own moral standard—whether it is the individual or collective—is nothing more than another example of relativism and carries with it dire consequences.

When two opposing moral viewpoints cross paths, they cannot exist as correct in the same space at the same time. Therefore, one of them, according to the Law of Non-Contradiction, must be correct and the other, incorrect. It may seem to be the case for some that if in some remote part of the world, a group of people participated in child sacrifices for entertainment, that it would be completely acceptable, as long they all agree it is acceptable. For most, what happens across the world in places we know little about, raises little concern. But when the airplanes slammed into the World Trade Center Towers in the name of justice for Islam, much of the rest of the world cried out, exclaiming a severe injustice and immoral act had taken place.

How then can those responsible for the deaths of over three thousand innocent lives be held accountable if we do not maintain some absolute moral standard? If we somehow choose ourselves to be the means by which we measure morality, then we are left with nothing to measure. For example, suppose that a little boy named Johnny had never seen a ruler, but was asked by his teacher, as a homework assignment, to go home and measure how tall he is. He looks around and decides to use himself to measure himself. The next day he arrives at school to turn his assignment in. He tells the teacher that he is one Johnny tall. Based on Johnny's assessment of how tall he is, do we have any real information on his actual height? Of course not. The measuring rod must be independent of the thing being measured; otherwise, we have nothing to measure.[71] The same holds true for morality.

What about the idea that morality is an intrinsic part of the universe? This idea still fails to address the origins of morality, how it is that people, over time, decide that a particular moral standard has changed, and does not explain how different cultures can have different moral perspectives. If moral authority is intrinsic, then we cannot affirm any kind of relative morality. Otherwise, what do we do with a culture or country that behaves in a fashion we might consider immoral? Two views of morality in direct opposition can't both be intrinsic.

For the Christian apologist, relative morality may seem to present a significant roadblock. After all, it sounds nice and relieves me of any responsibility to a higher standard of behavior. However, relative morality becomes a larger problem for the atheist. It should be clear now that humanity cannot be its own moral hero, nor can morality exist as some intrinsic understanding woven into the universe. That is unless you account for a Moral Law Giver. Without God, there is no moral standard. Without a moral standard, there are no means of measuring morality. Without the means which to measure morality, there is nothing left to measure. Therefore morals really do not exist.

As a result, the relativistic mindset is on a collision course for Nihilism or moral meaninglessness. "Since there is no objective moral meaning or value, there isn't any possibility of moral reasoning. Individuals are left to create 'morality' on the basis of anything or nothing."[72]

Therefore the atheist is unable to object to the killing of millions of Jews at the hands of Hitler, the rape of an innocent woman walking home from work, or the child gunned down in gang crossfire. All of it is meaningless without God. Theologian and professor, Michael Bird suggests that without a central reference point for our moral understanding,

> "Pushing an old lady in front of a bus is as equally meaningless as helping her walk across the street. We can collectively stipulate that such an action as wrong, but this is no more than an opinion that has no power or value beyond the subscription of a collective will. After all, on what basis or on what authority does one describe one deed as "good" and another deed as "evil"? In the absence of God, ethics is reduced to aesthetics."[73]

CONCLUSION

So what conclusion are we left with? Well, the cosmological evidence shows that he must be a supernatural power, for he is a power beyond nature who brought the whole natural world into existence. Also, he must be a superintelligence, for he designed a super-complex universe and human life. And he must be morally perfect, for he is the standard for all moral law. This is exactly what is meant by a theistic God."[74]

Once again it is important to stress that we cannot prove that

God exists beyond all doubt, short of the second coming of Christ. But is it reasonable to suggest, given all the evidence listed above, that, at a minimum, there is a Creator who designed this world, created it and gave it a set standard for conduct while on this earth? If we can say yes, then the existence of God is certainly the best possible explanation. But of course, there are many objections people have to believe in God, and these three primary arguments will help deal with most objections head-on.

When we are faced with, or experience a moment where we are confronted with the distinction between good and evil we have come face-to-face with God's divine image in us. It is about choosing justice over cruelty, compassion over pain, love over hate, and integrity over deception. It is about choosing to build another up, over tearing them down. However, seeing the world as such raises one of the most significant questions Christians ask. How can a good God allow so much evil in the world?

CONVERSATION STARTER

I want to be clear here. There is no smoking gun here. Students often expect it. There will always be objections, doubts, and discussion surrounding the existence of God. The key is to be prepared when those objections come. Below are some common objections. Discuss how to navigate them.

There is no proof of God.

Belief in God is nothing more than a psychological crutch.

Science can explain away any need for God.

CHAPTER ELEVEN

A PHILOSOPHICAL APPROACH TO EVIL AND SUFFERING

It is one of those events that have been burned in your memory—the morning that the World Trade Center Towers were rammed with commercial passenger jets. I remember because I heard about it on my drive into work that morning, but I didn't see the images until I arrived at work. It was as if time had frozen, yet we had to continue working. I was managing a restaurant that had over thirty televisions throughout the dining room. Should we turn off them off or just turn on ESPN? Do we talk about with customers or ignore it? I even had a server ask me if she should smile at her customers.

As the manager I duty I had to navigate a balance between a normal business flow and preparations for a lunch rush and recognition of the presence of evil being forced into our mundane world. We are all witnesses of evil in some way shape or form. Whether watching the horrific events unfold at Sandy Hook Elementary, the Orlando nightclub shooting, or the church in Charlottesville; or being the parent sitting helplessly at the bedside of a suffering child. We are inundated with stories and imagines that serve as a constant and often unwelcomed reminder of humanity's capacity for evil and the unnecessary suffering of so many people around the world.

It's times like these that tend to raise some of the most frequently asked questions about God's existence. Isn't God supposed to be so good and looks out for our best interests? Wouldn't someone we define as love never allow suffering? There are babies that die, natural disasters that kill hundreds of thousands of people, and senseless killings of others all over the world. If God were so good and powerful, then certainly He would have the capacity and desire to end such intense and useless suffering.

There two ways we can work through these questions of evil and suffering. One is looking into suffering as merely an intellectual or philosophical problem. The other is a personal experience and the emotion of pain and suffering or confronting evil first hand. Some people can simply think about suffering from an intellectual point of view and question God's goodness or even existence. But this is far different from those who have personally experienced suffering. The emotional pain often stands in the way of a person accepting the love of God and the healing power of the gospel. It is in these kinds of cases that our approach and relationship with people are more important than ever.

However, understanding evil at its roots philosophically, will inevitably lead to greater understanding of why an all-powerful, all-magnificent God would allow it. As difficult as it might be to grasp, the existence of evil provides us the very means by which we understand not only the all-encompassing goodness of God but also the very existence of Him. More simply, without the possibility of evil in our world, we would no doubt lack a proper understanding of the nature and character of God.

THE PHILOSOPHICAL PROBLEM

Up to this point, it would seem, at least, that all the evidence points to the existence of some kind of creator, sustainer, and designer. But when we add pain and suffering into the mix, it seems that all changes. The Greek philosopher, Epicurus—later reworded by David Hume—summarized what continues to be one of the most popular arguments against God.

If an all-powerful and perfectly good god exists, then evil does not.

There is evil in the world.

Therefore, an all-powerful and perfectly good god does not exist.

According to the atheist, if God were all-good, all-powerful, and all-perfect, then He would not only have the ability, but also the desire to stop the rampant evil and pain that haunts so many. Why would God not want to prevent a child from being born with a disability, or stop a natural disaster from killing hundreds of thousands of people? Often, the natural conclusion is that since He doesn't *always* prevent such evils, then He must not exist. Or at best, He is some kind of moral monster that people should run away from.

There is little doubt that the problem of evil and suffering haunts Christians and non-Christians alike. Many Christians have little to say regarding the purpose or reason for evil. No one can deny its existence, and so few seem to be able to explain why, if God exists, evil is allowed to disrupt, even ruin lives. So how can we account for and explain God's sovereignty in light of it? To answer these questions, we must first take a minute to be sure we have defined evil properly. As was the case with faith, truth, and reason, we need to be sure we are talking on the same plane as the person with whom we are engaged.

DEFINING EVIL

How would you define evil? Is it something that went horribly wrong with God's plan—a flaw? Or is evil something that God created? A clear definition of evil is difficult to nail down with any degree of certainty or agreement among scholars, both theistic and atheistic. When we speak of evil, we are generally speaking about the suffering caused by natural disasters, human disease, and moral wrongs committed against others. One specific side of evil is considered moral evil. These are morally evil acts willfully committed against other people. Otherwise known as the religious problem of evil—evil that arises from the experience of suffering and evil.[75] The problem of moral evil probes the question of why God, who is all-loving, would allow sin to enter the world.[76]

The other side of evil is considered natural evil. Natural disasters, illness, deformities, etc. describe those aspects of evil that are not directly caused by people against others, but that affect people for seemingly no reason or fault. Here there is no argument about what entails evil acts. It is the means by which, or origin, of evil that stirs up controversy.

Who is to blame for the child sold into slavery? Where is the justice for the woman who was raped? Why do tornadoes, tsunamis, and hurricanes rip through cities and towns and destroy people's lives at will? Who is to blame for these atrocities? And why do some disasters seem senselessly evil and unnecessary and others result in good?

It seems that most consider God to be the actual creator of evil, and is therefore to blame. If God were to exist, then He must be the originator of evil acts and natural disasters. The logic assumes that God created all things. Evil is a thing. Therefore, either God created evil, willingly decided to ignore it, or really can't do anything about it. Then why call him God?[77] If this is the case, then God could not be good and therefore could not exist. Further, why does God not prevent acts of gratuitous evil? Why not prevent senseless acts as widespread as the Holocaust or the trafficking of the teenage girl next door?

For Christian theism to work, God must be omnipresent (all-everywhere), omnipotent (all-powerful), omniscient (all-knowing), and omnibenevolent (all-good). If God is the creator of evil, then He might continue to be all-powerful, and all-everywhere, but would fail to be all-good. God would be reduced to the guy holding a lightening rod waiting for you to mess up and strike you down—waiting to punish you for the slightest mistake.

Among some of the more popular explanations comes from St. Augustine of Hippo (A.D. 354-430)[78], one of the most influential theologians in history. Augustine created an argument that illustrated evil as something that is not really a thing at all. He argued that evil is not a thing but the absence of good—a privation of good, and not a thing in itself. This idea is precisely how we measure light and heat. Darkness is not considered a thing, but the means by which we measure the absence of light. Cold and heat operate the same way. Cold is a descriptor for the lack of heat. Heat is the thing, not cold. Essentially, Augustine is saying that it is impossible for God to have created something that is actually nothing. Instead, God created good things. What comes from God must be good because God is inherently good. But even in creating humanity good and in His image, He also gave humanity free will. People have the ability to choose the absence of good and do evil. People have the ability to turn from God and choose evil.

EVIL ASSUMES A STANDARD

So to properly define evil, we need some kind of standard to compare it to. The fact that we recognize the existence of evil at any level presupposes a standard in which we judge what we consider to be evil. Michael Bird suggests that to deny God's existence due to evil and suffering is to make a self-defeating claim.[79] He notes,

> "It is possible to demonstrate that the argument from evil against God's existence presupposes precisely what it intends to refute. To believe that "evil" exists, one needs an absolute standard by which evil is judged to be, or else we are simply left with competing views and voices about who or what is evil."[80]

Without evil, there is no good, no standard for good and thus no need for God and ultimately no God at all. If our universe has no God, then good and evil do not exist. "...There is only the bare valueless fact of existence, and there is no one to say that you are right and I am wrong."[81] We know for sure that most people consider human trafficking to be morally wrong. How do we know this? What if God were able to wipe out human trafficking? What if He was somehow able to prevent people from engaging in such an immoral act? If no one ever committed such a crime, would we know it is wrong? Without a consistent standard, we lose our authority for how we call one deed good and another evil. Our ability to know wrong can only come from knowing the difference between right and wrong.

The great Christian apologist, Ravi Zacharias, explains the problem of evil as something which can actually prove the existence of God. He asserts (and rightfully, I would argue) that to declare there is evil in the world, one must assume there is something to compare that evil to, to call it evil. This comparison is defined as that which is good. So now there is a clear distinction made between what is good and what is evil. If one claims there is a distinction between the two, then there must be a standard to be used to make the distinction. If there is a standard, then there is a moral law, if there is a moral law, then there must be a giver of the moral law. Consequently, we find ourselves right back to the morality argument for the existence of God.

If then, the atheist is going to claim that evil does in fact exist, then the Christian would be compelled to agree; and rightly so. But to claim that evil exists, one must then claim that good exists, because evil is a corrupted good. C.S. Lewis stated it this way:

> "You can be good for the mere sake of goodness; you cannot be bad for the mere sake of badness You can do a kind action when you are not feeling kind and when it gives you no pleasure, simply because kindness is right; but no one ever did a cruel action simply because cruelty is wrong—only because cruelty was pleasant or useful to him...Goodness is, so to speak itself; badness is only spoiled goodness. And there must be something good before it can be spoiled."[82]

The only logical conclusion left for the atheist is that evil no longer exists. And if evil no longer exists in the objective sense, we are left with nothing more than moral nihilism. We are left speaking a moral language reduced to an arbitrary system of values and beliefs void of any ontological grounds for prescription.[83] So to the atheist who claims that God cannot exist because of all the evil in the world, the Christian can say that because we know there is evil in the world, then God must exist. It is only by God's perfect goodness that we can know the difference between what is good and what is evil.

MORAL FREE WILL

But if God can get the world in motion, make the stars, and create such complex creatures with the ability to love, then why not set it up so that people, in the face of evil, would choose to do right? If God is so powerful, then why can't He make a world so good that people don't want to do evil, or the means to do evil are no longer available? God can do anything, right? In Sunday school, children boldly proclaim, "my God is so great, so strong and so mighty, there is nothing my God cannot do." But is there *nothing* God cannot do?

There are a few things that God cannot do. He cannot do things that contradict His character, He cannot cease to exist, He cannot create a square circle, He cannot suddenly make 2+2 equal 5, and He cannot create people to do whatever He wants. God can create free creatures, but He cannot cause or determine them to only do things that are morally right. But God does work within the free nature of humanity, and the evil that does exist, in order to bring about the best possible good.[84]

Taking into consideration an action that is morally significant (a decision to murder, rather than a decision on what to wear), and that a person is significantly free (not forced to commit an act against their will), Notre Dame professor and philosopher, Alvin Plantinga notes that, "a world containing creatures who are significantly free (and freely perform more good than evil actions) is more valuable, all else being equal than a world containing no free creatures at all."[85] If God were to create somehow a world where people were predetermined in their actions to do good, then freedom would cease to exist. "To create creatures capable of moral good, therefore, he must create creatures capable of moral evil; and he can't give these creatures the freedom to perform evil and at the same time prevent them from doing so."[86]

This, however, does not mean that evil must exist in order for there to be morally free creatures; Plantinga only states that evil must remain as a possibility, leaving room for good to overcome evil, and people have the ability to choose good freely. In other words, if humanity truly has the freedom to choose every possible action, then every possible action must include possible evil actions. Eliminating even one choice eliminates free will.

Therefore it is possible that an all-good, all-powerful, and all-knowing God can exist alongside the presence of evil. The existence of pain and suffering or the degree of pain and suffering has no bearing on whether or not God exists. We know that the absence of good provides a place for evil, we know that the only way we know what is good is because we identify what is evil, and finally, the only means by which people can be morally free agents who have the ability to do good, is if we have the ability to do evil. Of course, this is all very philosophical and, to be honest, may not be enough for the person who has been directly impacted by pain and suffering whether through moral or natural evil. This argument only covers moral evil or acts committed willfully by one person to another. What about natural disasters, terminal illnesses, and birth defects?

When we talk about the problem of evil, we tend to focus on the problem of moral evil. But what deserves an equal amount of attention is the problem of natural evil. Why does God allow suffering as a result of natural occurrences, disease, and illness? We know from Genesis 1 that God created a world perfect in goodness and order. Original sin, however, disrupted this order and perfection—not so much our ongoing sin, but the sin of Satan's initial rebellion and the sin of Adam and Eve. Now it could be possible that God could have created a world that was static and unaffected by this sin, however, doing so would have similar effects to God creating morally free creatures unable to commit acts of evil. In his formulation of what is known as the Free Process Defense, Garrett DeWeese states,

> "Now if natural evil were not possible in an analogous parallel world, it also would be a world in which natural science, engineering, even education would be vacuous. Courage and excitement would be absent since no real harm would occur. A careful structural design would be meaningless since no earthquake or tornado would destroy homes or buildings. Medical arts would be nonexistent since disease would not harm or kill. It would not be a world worthy of rational, creative agents, even if it was a world that was livable."[87]

If God created a world in which the potential for moral evil existed, but not the actual evil, then the same holds true for natural evil. In His creating a dynamic world of creativity, God only created the potential for natural evil, not the natural evil itself. God did not create the AIDS virus, but only the potential for it to exist. Likewise, God did not create the earthquake, but only the potential for tectonic plates to shift given the right conditions to cause such an event. In His omniscience, God still knows if and when these events are going to occur, but in that same omniscience decided to design the world in such a fashion.[88] Yet within such disaster is the potential for the image of God in man—through humanity's creativity—to bring healing, rebuilding, and restoration—all images of the kingdom to come.

CONCLUSION

When we think of God and evil, it is important to note, that when we say that God allows evil, what we are really saying is that God, in His perfect creative plan, allowed for the gift of free will. However, in that free will, man chose to commit evil acts. Because in a world that is truly free, there must be the potential for truly free beings to commit acts of evil as well as acts of good. In Adam's act of disobedience, we caught a glimpse of evil and what it can do to humanity and the rest of creation. However, we also caught a glimmer of God's grace and goodness. And it was God, in His perfect omniscience, knew that Adam would slip up; and by doing so, provided a way that light would be best seen in the darkness. In other words, the suffering is our fault, and since our rebellion could not simply be excused, Jesus died for rebellious humans.

In the world, as it is, evil is unavoidable. However, in the meantime, we labor on earth, bringing goodness, light, and the beauty of God into our midst—our families, workplaces, and neighborhoods. Those who trust God while navigating severe evil and suffering are learning to overcome evil with good. To be a part of God's kingdom requires that we use our free will rightly in our reigning with Jesus for eternity. Essentially, evil and suffering in our world becomes the proving grounds of a faith, of greater worth than gold, that is tested, refined, and purified.

As God does so frequently and so well, He took what was evil and what tainted humanity and worked it for our good and used it to draw us closer to Him. It is the process by which we make ourselves nothing so that Jesus can become something greater.

CONVERSATION STARTER

The question of evil continues to be the number one question among students—in large part because the problem of evil affects all people on all kinds of fronts.

How would explain or help a person struggling with pain, suffering, or the presence of evil in their lives?

CHAPTER TWELVE
THE PERSONAL REALITY OF PAIN

Several years ago when my oldest daughter was just four-years-old, we were spending some time outside at a nature center. It was one of those mild, damp days midwestern springs are known for. We were walking near a small pond, and without warning, my daughter started screaming. Something had caused her to be terrified. As I looked around, it took me a minute to notice the swarms of gnats flying in our midst. She didn't like bugs to begin with, but she had yet to experience so many in one place at one time. Although small in scope to me, she was experiencing something terrifying and evil.

She felt threatened. She felt as though she would be hurt. She grabbed on to me and held me tighter than she ever had before. I didn't have to remove her from what she thought was going to hurt her; I just had to hold her. In her small four-year-old mind, she had no plan for what I should do, or how holding on to me tightly would help; she only knew that in my arms there was rescue, safety, and security. Her only answer to her fear and suffering was to hold tight, put her face on my shoulder and wait for it to be over. It is here that our argument must shift from the philosophical to the theological—from the logical arguments to the pastoral conversation

THE EXISTENTIAL PROBLEM

As we noted in the last chapter, when the world was created, God created everything good. He made a universe that was perfectly good. Everything was as it should be. After God was done with creating everything, something happened that reduced the good in the world—a loss of good and the entrance of evil. Now, remember that from a philosophical point of view, evil is necessary and that it can enhance our case for God's existence. For the atheist who wishes to disprove God by suggesting the problem of evil as proof, he has lost ground in his argument. Further, we also learned that man has moral free will. So, if God is good and all he created is good, then is it possible that some of the greatest possible good can come from evil?

Our moral free will allows us the opportunity to reflect the true nature and character of our Creator—the nature of love. Without free will, there is no conceivable way we could love God or accept the love He offers back to His creation, without becoming some sort of puppets or robots designed to operate on command. Out of such a love comes some of the greatest good the world could imagine, including the gospel. But is it worth all of the trouble, all of the pain, just to see some good in the world? If there were no evil, would we know any different? Without evil, what things might we not be able to experience? What about acts of forgiveness, or mercy, long-suffering, and heroism? All of these would cease to exist.

When evil disrupts our lives—even though God did not necessarily cause the evil—he uses it to draw us into his arms for rescue and comfort. God desires for us to rest in Him and often it is in the deepest moments of pain and suffering that we come to Him more willingly, and we come to know Him more intimately. When we have the opportunity to come alongside someone who is suffering, we want to avoid the philosophical and bad theological arguments like those of Job's friends (Job 8, 11, 15, 18, 20, 22), refrain from searching for answers, and simply help them see the face of God through you. Job, blameless in the eyes of God, took a roller coaster of emotions and bad advice only to be reminded that at the center of his suffering is God teaching something. Job never learns why he is suffering, but what he does learn is that it is never about the suffering or why there is suffering, or even why he suffered the way he did. Instead, it is about God. It is not about why, but who. It is about God who is holding you as you move through suffering. It is in the dark that the light shines the brightest.

In the face of what appears to be a dismal world, filled with pain and suffering caused by rampant evil, it doesn't take much to conclude that if there is a Creator, then He simply is mean and unjust. Many Christians and non-Christians alike assume that if God put us here on earth and created the world for us to live in, then it seems to make sense that the greatest good is our immediate sense of personal pleasure and satisfaction. Therefore, if there is some circumstance in which we cannot have immediate satisfaction, then God must either have abandoned us, not exist or be evil for allowing us to experience any discomfort. But again, this has to do with our view of who God is. If God denies our immediate gratification, then we have to assume there is a good reason for doing so. The character and plan of God provides a long-term solution to the problem of evil and suffering. That plan was Christ on the cross and the resurrection that followed. It was God's plan to fulfill His promise and rescue His creation, and decisively end the problem of evil and suffering.

In the meantime, humans are morally responsible for their actions. We can choose good, obedience, and righteousness; or we can choose defiance, rebellion, and evil. As believers in Jesus, Christians can face pain and suffering head-on with joy because of the realization of the hope of the resurrection that waits on the other side. This is precisely the point that Peter makes to a church filled with followers of Jesus enduring evil and suffering at the hands of the Roman Empire.

"Praise be to the God and Father of our Lord Jesus Christ! In his great mercy, he has given us new birth into a living hope through the resurrection of Jesus Christ from the dead, and into an inheritance that can never perish, spoil or fade. This inheritance is kept in heaven for you, who through faith are shielded by God's power until the coming of the salvation that is ready to be revealed in the last time. In all this, you greatly rejoice, though now for a little while you may have had to suffer grief in all kinds of trials. These have come so that the proven genuineness of your faith—of greater worth than gold, which perishes even though refined by fire—may result in praise, glory, and honor when Jesus Christ is revealed. Though you have not seen him, you love him; and even though you do not see him now, you believe in him and are filled with an inexpressible and glorious joy, for you are receiving the end result of your faith, the salvation of your souls." - 1 Peter 1:3-9

Evil does something different for the Christian. It ushers in a unique opportunity for the image and rule of Christ here on earth to be made known. When people see Christians' correct response to suffering—a response of joy—they will see the image of Christ. God may not be able to prevent evil and the pain and suffering that ensues, but through the ultimate suffering of Jesus on the cross, He has provided the means to deal with it. Because of the resurrection, those who follow Jesus have the assurance of the promise of God to redeem all of creation and set everything back to rights. In the meantime, Jesus has called his followers to be the joy, be the resurrection, be the light, and be the means by which the Holy Spirit brings people back to the Father.

> "And we know that in all things God works for the good of those who love him, who have been called according to his purpose." - Romans 8:28

It may not always look as though He is, but He is working for our good. It is not necessarily an individual good, or an immediate good, or even the good we perceive we need. The good that God is working towards is the good that comes from His promise of redemption, restoration and rest, and the good comes from the inexpressible and glorious joy, for you are receiving the outcome of your faith, the salvation of your souls (1 Peter 1:9).

BUT WHAT ABOUT...?

Why does God allow a child to die? This, of course, is a tremendously difficult and often very personal question. So often instead of the general question, why does God let a child die, is the more personal question, why did God allow my child to die? While the latter question is much more difficult, it is the former that provides the necessary context and answers for why any child dies. There is no doubt nobody wants to see a child suffer or die at any time for any reason. But reality tells a much different story. The reality is that the death that Adam's sin ushered in does not discriminate. God told Adam that death was now a part of life, but he didn't say when death would happen, how it would happen, or who; only that death was the result of his sin.

To state it simply, sin is destructive. The sheer fact that we hate watching a child suffer speaks to our deep need for Jesus. Although God promised that death was the unavoidable consequence of sin, He also promised redemption and restoration. When we see the child who lays in a hospital bed suffering and facing death, we reach for some kind of hope in the midst of such a tragedy. Now imagine such a tragedy without the reality of Jesus or the truth of the gospel. With Jesus, there remains hope. Without him, there is no hope, because there is no other side to death. There is only death. The grim reality is, is that without God, we cannot even ask the question. A child's death is certainly tragic in every scenario. But it is even more tragic, without God waiting on the other side of the tragedy.

However, this forces us to return to the question of God's ability to intervene. "Can't God just stop sin and its effects?" One would think that an all-powerful God would possess the ability to orchestrate humanity in such a way that benefits all. Therefore, the horrible realities of this world, like the suffering and death of children would cease to be a part of our reality. As utopian and idealistic as this sounds, part of the beauty of creation is the freedom to choose. God did not create robotic creatures that could be ordered, programmed or manipulated to do the bidding of their master. Remember that humanity can choose good and therefore also can choose evil. There is incredible beauty and perfection in God's choice to give us free will, but unfortunately, He has to leave room for the ugliness of rebellion and evil. But without the goodness of God and the life he offers, we can't understand the horror and evil of a suffering child. Our free will offers us the knowledge of what is good and what is evil. Without it, we would never understand the difference

Why do bad things happen to good people? The problem here is that this is the wrong question. Rather than asking the question, "why do bad things happen to good people?" One should simply ask, "why to bad things happen to people?" Technically speaking, people are not *good.* God created humans with free will and gave them paradise. As we have already discovered, God could not have created creatures with the free ability only to choose good. Without the ability to choose evil, how do we know what is good? Our finite minds, even though reflective of God, still need to understand a standard or origin for good and evil. Therefore, evil is allowed to exist, so that we can be truly free creatures. But humanity distrusted God and rebelled against Him thus bringing immense suffering on themselves and others. Since their rebellion could not simply be excused, Jesus died for a rebellious humanity. Now, humans who trust God learn the horror of rebellion through experiencing rebellion's devastating results. They also learn to overcome evil with good. This knowledge prepares them to be inheritors of God's kingdom where they will use their free will rightly in their reigning with Jesus forever and ever.

We live in a world where bad things happen to all people. Period. People can freely choose to do something good, or do something evil. I can either hurt or help another. So long as humanity has the ability to choose evil, many will and, therefore, affect the lives of many others. Mankind's exercise in their freedoms have caused the evil, and to maintain our freedom, God must allow and consequently deal with it as the sole authority and judge of moral behavior.

Why did God in the Old Testament command evil, like the killing of Canaanite children? It is often very easy for us to cry out in rage against God for the commanded killing of all the Canaanites as Israel took the Promised Land. After all, this speaks directly to the perceived character of God. Of course, this is genocide, infanticide, and downright appalling to think of God—said to be all loving—ends up destroying entire people groups based on nothing more than feeling or preference for one people group over another. Or so the argument tends to go. However, as legitimate as this objection may sound, when put in context and all factors are taken into account, a tamer picture begins to emerge, and God is exonerated from the charge of such heinous crimes.

First, we need to consider the people who occupied the land of Canaan. The degree to which these people were in sin far exceeds most of our modern understanding. Their culture was rampant with severe sexual sin, child molestation and the sacrificing of children. Additionally, the Canaanites were given every chance to flee the region, or, at least, send the women and children to safety, in which many certainly did, and yet others remained and suffered as a result. It is also important to remember this was a time of ancient war. Now, of course, it sounds very philanthropic to assert that someone should have—whatever the cost—worked to save the children. After all, they are just kids. Wouldn't God look that much better as a humanitarian, saving the women and children, and have them brought up as an Israelite?

However, despite how pleasant, such an act looks on the surface, we have no means of accurately predicting the outcome for those children. What might happen if these children whom the Israelites saved found out that their adopted parents killed their real parents? Further, how much of the Canaanite cultural influence remained with these children? The point here is that there are so many unknown factors and circumstances, and yet we assume we know more than God who is supposed to be all-powerful, all-knowing, and completely sovereign.

Second, if God is truly all-powerful, all-knowing, and completely sovereign, then he would, of course, know the pattern of choices these children would be making throughout their life, whether in the culture of Canaan, or Israel. Therefore, any execution of such children would be justified. If we argue that God cannot know such things, and therefore, does not have the right to order the execution of children, then he is less than what is considered God and therefore, lacks the authority and ability to give such an order.

Lastly, we do not know the eternal fate of these children. Often this objection is met with the assumption that since these children do not *know* God in the sense that Christians often assume, then there is an automatic assumption that these children were not only unjustifiably murdered, but will also spend an eternity in hell for a crime they had no idea they were committing. However, these are all nothing more than mere assumptions. Frankly, we might as well assume these children are spending an eternity in the Kingdom of Heaven, enjoying an existence far better than the life that awaited them in Canaan.

Although it is immensely difficult to imagine any justified killing of any child for any reason, we must gather and consider all the facts of a place and time far different than today.

CONCLUSION

Pain and suffering is a genuine reality for many. But God did not create the evil that causes it—evil is not a thing to be created. Instead, in our free will, we have the ability to commit acts that reflect the absence of good, which can harm others as well as ourselves. This privation of good can, in fact, serve the purposes of God, as it can point us back to Him, as well as offer good to be shown in light of evil.

Logically speaking, the problem of evil is no problem at all for the Christian. Instead, the problem lies with the atheist. If there is no God, then any basis for objective standards of right and wrong (the very tool we use to determine what is evil and what is not) is eliminated. Moral values and evil are reduced to personal taste or through the evolution of cultural ideals and conditioning. Further, if God does not exist, then the evil deeds of by man are left unchecked. No solution, no comfort, and no redemption are offered to the human plight. Consequently, just as the case with morality, humanity is headed toward the same inevitable result—nihilism, or nothingness and meaninglessness. Friedrich Nietzsche said God is dead. The proper response is, "If God is dead, then man is dead too."[89]

However, it is vital for us to understand that many times when people bring up the issue of evil, there is a deeper issue, a deeper pain within that person. Often we find that, instead of looking to make the best possible case or trying to prove our point, we must simply address the greater need of being Christ to that person. We must show them a God who loves, wishes to heal, and wishes to begin a new creation in that person, and we have the opportunity and privilege to be a part of that redemption process.

CONVERSATION STARTER

The previous chapter dealt with the academic or philosophical problem. This chapter dialed in, in more detail how the presence of evil affects people. Students may still struggle with why God allows pain and suffering—especially if they have gone through something painful. Be sure to spend the necessary time talking with them.

What questions do you still have regarding why God allows evil?

CHAPTER THIRTEEN
CAN THE NEW TESTAMENT BE TRUSTED?

"Doesn't the Bible just give us great moral stories and lesson to learn from?" "If I believe in Jesus, go to church, and call myself a Christian, what value does the Bible really have?" "The Bible is so old, isn't it outdated and irrelevant for modern culture?" In over a decade of teaching the Bible in the classroom, these questions—or some version of—were asked by my students every year and in every class, without fail.

Whether it is the fluidity of our culture's moral guidelines, the lack of evidence for modern day miracles, or simply the difficulty believing the Bible to be a document inspired by God and infallible in its message, students are finding it easier and easier to dismiss the reliability of the Bible. This, of course, presents a somewhat unique challenge in teaching our students the Christian worldview. We can spend all the time in the world explaining evidence from nature, from science, and even from logic that God is the creator; but it is the biblical story that informs our understanding of who God is and how He interacts with history. And it is the New Testament that introduces us to the fundamental foundation for what Christians believe—Jesus Christ.

Given the challenges of our culture and its indoctrination of Generation Z, it is more important than ever that our students not only grab hold of the truth found in Scripture but are confident of its reliability and authority for the truth it proclaims.

For my students, it wasn't enough to assume the Bible was the Word of God, just because pastor said so. And it certainly wasn't enough to believe the Bible is inspired and infallible because the Bible said so. If they were going to study the words and actions of Jesus, they needed to be sure that these stories were more than just ancient myths. Could the Bible—specifically the New Testament—serve as a reliable source for truth, morality, and our entire understanding of Jesus life and ministry? To put it more simply: Is the Bible all that it is cracked up to be? And if so, how can I be sure?

CRITICISM LEVELED AGAINST CHRISTIANS

As I said above, it isn't enough anymore to claim the truth and authority of Jesus' words on the authority of the Bible itself. Skeptics (and students for that matter) quickly pick up on the circular reasoning, making it all the more reasonable to claim that the Bible is inconsistent and unreliable, and not at all in line with historical facts. Atheists across a broad spectrum have made clear the supposed fallacies Scripture presents. Well known atheist philosopher, Bertrand Russell commented, *"Historically it is quite doubtful whether Christ ever existed at all, and if he did we do not know anything about him."*[90] Others have duly noted the circular reasoning some Christians resort to. *"You say you believe in the Bible because of Jesus, but then you say you believe in Jesus because of the Bible. This is circular reasoning."* Still, others cite the countless translations and copies as the inevitable path to making of great stories of legend.

Were my students right in asking the question? Were they right to question—even completely doubt—the Bible's reliability and authority? Can we know for sure the Scriptures, especially the New Testament, are a reliable source for what Christians claim about God, salvation, truth, and the fate of humanity? Can we know if what we hold in our hands has been translated correctly and copied accurately from the historical events?

Yes, that is a lot of questions. Fortunately, there are plenty of answers that get to the heart of what all of our students—and even us—are asking when it comes to the Bible. It is unreasonable to assume that any of us would just accept the Bible as the Word of God without reason to do so. Likewise, we can't expect our students to submit to its authority if we don't provide them legitimate reasons to do so. These next two chapters will aim to address precisely these issues. While not completely exhaustive, you will have enough information and training to ease the worried minds of your students and challenge even the most ardent of skeptics.

UNDERSTANDING TRANSLATION

The issue of translation haunts many Christians because we often have no idea how to address it. Some church traditions have asserted that a particular translation is the only "correct" translation, others teach about Jesus from a paraphrased Bible such as *The Message*. There are even churches that have eliminated the use of the Bible altogether, to appear more relevant to an increasingly skeptical audience.

If you were to enter any local Christian bookstore and wander the aisle with all the Bibles, it would not be long before you noticed and even became confused by all the different translations. There are dozens in English alone and hundreds when you throw in other languages. With so many translations, it is no wonder people doubt the reliability of the Bible. What is the point of all of them? How can I explain it all to someone else? Is one better or more accurate than another?

To help sort this out, we can easily classify the translations into a few categories, each working to accomplish a specific purpose while holding to the true meaning of the original Scriptures.

First, some translations are designed to be as literal as possible. In this case, translators attempt to render the Greek and Hebrew text word for word as much as possible, taking into account the cultural traditions and customs of biblical times. These can be hard to read at times but are thought to be the most accurate or closest to the original language and meaning (Examples: NASB, NIV, KJV).

Second, are the translations aimed at the author's intention. Here translators take what they think the authors meant and work the text into more familiar, modern language to connect the reader to the text in a more meaningful, relevant way. Reading these types of Bibles is greatly dependent on the accuracy of the translators in their assessment of what the text means and how it should be translated into modern language (Example: The New Living Translation or NLT, Amplified Bible). Finally, Eugene Peterson wrote *The Message*. He did an excellent job of taking the words of Scripture and its teaching and creating almost a commentary for the lay Christian. Some think it is more interesting and therefore more readable. This, in turn, could create a greater chance of the person actually reading the Bible. It is important to note that *The Message* is not considered the inspired Word of God as the other translations are, although it conveys the same truth.

Of course, if you want to get serious you could learn Greek and Hebrew and just read the original text. However, this still does not eliminate many issues the translators face. You still must translate an ancient document in an ancient culture into modern English in modern culture.

The issue is not just that there are so many different kinds of translations. It is also in understanding how those translations ought to be interpreted in light of the context of the ancient world. Every ancient document, biblical or not, has to be translated from one language to another. The difficulty lies in bridging the gaps that exist in language, culture, and even style of literature.

WHY ARE WE NOT ARGUING IN A CIRCLE?[91]

Even if we can prove that the documents we have today reflect the ancient writings and exercise extreme care and substantial scholarship when interpreting those documents; that still does not make them correct. If we are using only the Bible to prove that Jesus existed and that he was who he said he was and it is the Bible that tells us this, then, yes, this is circular reasoning unless you can show the Bible to be an authoritative, objective source for information. Let me show you what I mean.

> If God exists, then miracles are possible. If we are asserting the claim that God exists, then we are arguing the possibility that He is all-powerful, all-knowing, etc. Therefore we can affirm the possibility of miracles.

The New Testament documents are historically reliable. The New Testament documents are an accurate record of actual historical events. In other words, the things recorded happened the way they were recorded, including the words and actions of Jesus of Nazareth.

In the New Testament, Jesus claimed to be God. It is unmistakably clear that Jesus makes the claim to be the one and true God, the creator of everything.

Jesus proved to be God by an unprecedented convergence of miracles. Jesus' life and ministry illustrate the miracle of fulfilled prophecy, and most notably, the miracle of the Resurrection.

Therefore, Jesus was God in human flesh.

What Jesus (who is God) teaches is true.

Jesus taught the Bible is the Word of God.

Therefore the Bible is the Word of God.

However, everything in this proof hinges on two things. First, God exists. If you cannot get there, showing that the Bible is a reliable source document ends up a waste of time. Second, we must prove the Bible is a reliable source document, not a book of stories, fables, and contradictions.

Consequently, many questions surround this claim that needs to be addressed. How do you know the Bible has been accurately translated from the original? Couldn't the writers have accurately recorded a bunch of lies? How do we know that the Bible is not just a myth that developed over time? Are the New Testament documents a reliable record of the things Jesus said and did?

THE RELIABILITY OF THE NEW TESTAMENT

Think for a moment about the history students study in school. Where does all that information come from? What are the source documents and are those materials a reliable source of historical events? How can we know what is recorded about Alexander the Great, or Julius Ceaser is not mythical? There are three specific ways or tests we can to use to show just how trustworthy ancient documents are. These tests will help us discover how the New Testament stacks up against the rest of what we have from antiquity. In other words, is the New Testament a good source document for the claims of the Christian worldview compared to other documents of the same or similar period?

Bibliographical Test: This examines the textual transmission by which documents reach us. So if we took all the copies we have from different time periods and different locations, how many do we have and how does that number compare to other documents of a similar period? The chart below (figure 1) gives us several writings from various authors. Look closely at the right two columns. Not only do you want the greatest number of copies, but you also want to smallest gap from autograph to manuscript. This is the time between the original writing and the first known copy of the book—the smaller the gap, the more reliable the text.[92]

We have nearly six thousand handwritten Greek New Testament manuscripts. Additionally, more than ten thousand copies of the

Latin Vulgate, the Latin translation of the Bible, ninety-three hundred copies in Old Latin, Slavic, Arabic, Anglo Saxon, and other languages for a total of more than 25,000 manuscript copies of portions of the New Testament exist today. And this number continues to grow. When the numbers of Greek manuscripts are compared to the rest of the known literature of the ancient world, the evidence is staggering. The reliability of the New Testament far outweighs the rest of ancient world's documents.

Author	Book	Gap from autograph to manuscript	Number of copies
Caesar	Gallic Wars	950 years	251
Plato	Tetralogies	c. 1300 years	210
Tacitus	Annals	750-950 years	33
Pliny	Natural History	c. 750 years	200
Thucydides	History	c. 1300 years	96
Herodotus	History	c. 1350 years	109
Homer	Iliad	c. 400 years	1,757
New Testament		25-100 years	5,795

Figure 1[93]

If the sheer vastness of manuscripts copies wasn't enough, figure 2 takes the evidence even further. The New Testament has earlier manuscripts that are closer to the time of the original composition than any other major document of its time. For example, residing in the John Rylands Library in Manchester, England is what is known to be the oldest manuscript copy of any New Testament document. Known as the John Rylands fragment, this group of papyri is portions of John's Gospel dated somewhere between 117-138 A.D. Making this manuscript only one generation removed from the original autograph by the Apostle John.

Dated only a few years later is what is known as the Bodmer Papyrus (150-200 A.D.). This is a group of twenty-two papyri discovered in Egypt. In this group are segments of Old and New Testament as well as near complete portions of the New Testament. Similarly, is the Chester Beatty Papyri (250 A.D.), containing most of the New Testament and the Codex Vaticanus (325-350 A.D.), including almost the entire Bible.

Once again if compared to the rest of the ancient world, the Bible has more evidence and more accurate evidence than any other document of its time. Even with more than twenty-five thousand New Testament manuscripts, they are so similar that we are virtually certain of 97-98% of the New Testament. The remaining 2-3% account for one or two-word variants in the manuscripts. These variants are things like spelling, adding "the," etc., and yet none of these affect doctrine.[94] The evidence for the accuracy of the New Testament is some of the best we have for giving good reasons for Christian truth. Theologian Bruce Metzger is right,

> "The works of several ancient authors are preserved to us by the thinnest possible thread of transmission …in contrast …the textual critic of the New Testament is embarrassed by the wealth of his material."[95]

Author	Book	Written	Earliest Copy	Gap from Autograph to Manuscript
Caesar	Gallic Wars	100-44 BC	9th century	950 years
Plato	Tetralogies	400 BC	AD 895	c. 1300 years
Tacitus	Annals	100 AD	c. AD 1100	750-950 years
Pliny	Natural History	AD 49-79	14th-15th century	c. 750 years
Thucydides	History	460-400 BC	AD 900	c. 1300 years
Herodotus	History	480-425 BC	c. 900 AD	c. 1350 years
Homer	Iliad	800 BC	c. 400 BC	c. 400 years
New Testament		**50-100 AD**	**c. 114 fragments** **c. 200 books** **c. 250 most of NT** **c. 325 completed**	**25-50 years** **100 years** **150 years** **225 years**

Figure 2

The conclusion is simple. Throw out the New Testament as an unreliable source for history, filled with nothing more than contradictions, false accounts of miracles, and careless copying; and you are forced to throw out every other piece of history in the ancient world with it. When placed alongside the history of the first century, the New Testament documents make the most reliable information available. To ignore it would not only be intellectually dishonest, but dangerous.

External evidence test: External evidence determines whether other historical material confirms or denies the internal testimony of the document. In other words, we look to sources outside of the Bible to see if the historical record of the biblical narrative aligns with other ancient historians. We can find several comments made by Roman and Jewish historians about followers of Jesus, Christianity as a disturbance or cult, etc. This gives us evidence that what is in Scripture aligns with recorded secular history, as well as telling us that, at minimum, first-century Christians believed Jesus resurrected. While these documents do not prove anything independently, when taken with other evidence it helps tremendously with building our cumulative case. For example Flavius Josephus, a Jewish historian born around the time of Jesus' death who chronicled much of Roman history has provided important insight into the first-century Roman and Jewish world. His most famous works are the *Jewish War* and *Jewish Antiquities*.

> "At this time there was a wise man who was called Jesus. And his conduct was good and (he) was known to be virtuous. And many people from among the Jews and other nations became his disciples. Pilate condemned him to be crucified and to die. And those who had become his disciples did not abandon his discipleship. They reported that he had appeared to them three days after his crucifixion and that he was alive; accordingly, He was perhaps the Messiah concerning whom the prophets have recounted wonders." – *Jewish Antiquities*

Internal evidence test: This test determines whether (or to what extent) the written record is credible and attempts to gauge the author's ability to tell the truth. Here we are dealing with two specific objections. First, the large number of contradictions in the text reveals authors who are either making up stories, or chose to intentionally lie. Many people read parts of the Bible and claim that there are too many contradictions to be sure what the writers are saying is true, or that the writers of Scripture chose only to benefit themselves or their cause. Second, the biblical authors had good reason or motivation to lie about what they recorded. So let's consider these objections.

The witnesses or writers did not contradict each other. What then do we do with discrepancies that people bring up? Consider the following: In Matthew 27:5 we read that Judas "hanged himself." However in Acts 1:18, Luke seems to contradict Matthew's account: "... falling headlong, he burst open in the middle, and all his entrails gushed out."

What often seems like a contradiction requires a simple solution. Dr. Norman Geisler suggests that "sometime after hanging himself, his body was discovered, the rope cut, and the body fell on sharp rocks and burst open." Instead of a problem, we have two perspectives on one story. For example, if a police officer were required to record the events of an accident, he would not ask only one witness for an account of the accident. Good police work would require the officer to gather as much information from as many witnesses as possible. This would re-create the best possible scenario and provide the most information about what happened at the scene. The same could be said of the gospel accounts of Jesus. So the fact that we have different accounts regarding the same event strengthens our case for its truth.

Secondly, there were a sufficient number of witnesses. This was not just some guy writing down a bunch of teachings he thought was important or that he liked. There are nine different people who wrote the New Testament, all of whom were eyewitnesses or contemporaries to the events they recorded. Six of the witnesses are the most important to establishing Jesus' claim of miracles (Matthew, Mark, Luke, John, Acts, and Paul's letter to the Corinthians), all of which bear witness to the miracle of the Resurrection. Further, Paul states in 1 Corinthians 15—arguably, the earliest written record of the resurrection witnesses—that there were 500 people who saw Jesus after the Resurrection.

Finally, we can contend that the witnesses were truthful. Most of them died for how they lived and what they taught about Christ (2 Timothy 4:6-8; 2 Peter 1:14). Christians were greatly persecuted in the early days of the church. So if this was all just a hoax, and Jesus never really resurrected, how can we explain the commitment of each of the apostles—a commitment that led them each to a horrible death. In other words, they had no motivation to lie about what they wrote. In fact, it is more likely they would have lied to the contrary.

According to church tradition, all the disciples suffered a gruesome death as a martyr. While we can't be completely certain of the means of these deaths, we do know they suffered as a result of what they believed, preached about, and lived. It has been said that Peter's brother, Andrew was crucified and then hanged on an olive tree in Patrae, a town in Achaia. Bartholomew (Nathanael) was known to be the first to proclaim Jesus as the Son of God (John 1:49). Tradition says he was later told to recant his belief in Jesus. When he refused, he was beaten to death with clubs and then crucified. The Apostle John is thought to be the only apostle to have died from natural causes. He did, however, live the life of a martyr. He was exiled to the island of Patmos under Emperor Domitian. Church tradition records that he was thrown into boiling oil was not killed but severely wounded.

Throughout his missionary journeys, Paul suffered prison, beatings, being shipwrecked, and ended with his beheading in Rome under Emperor Nero in 67 A.D. When Peter denied Jesus three times at Jesus' crucifixion, it would be the last time he ever denied his Lord.

Peter, as Roman executioners prepared him for crucifixion, he thought himself unworthy to be crucified in the same manner as his Lord. So he asked to be crucified upside down. According to Acts 12:2, James, the brother of John was arrested by King Herod and was "put to death by the sword."

The witnesses to the resurrection had nothing to gain personally. They were persecuted and threatened with death for their belief in the gospel (cf. Acts 4, 5, 8). They even wrote things that didn't necessarily reflect favorably on them or their cause. For example, the disciples argued about positions of honor in heaven and who would have a seat at Jesus' right hand (Mt. 20: 21); Peter, at one point, chose to not eat with those who were uncircumcised and Paul rebuked him (Gal. 2:11-12); women found the tomb empty first (Mt. 28:7-8; Mark 16:5-6; Luke 24:3; Jn. 20:1-2); and Jesus even called Peter, "Satan" (Mt. 16:23).

THE SKEPTICS RESPONSE

Despite all of this overwhelming evidence, the skeptic may still hold the position that the Bible is filled with contradictions. They might claim that the gospel accounts of Jesus cannot be trusted because they are so different and that Paul contradicts Jesus and James. What about the other "gospels" like Thomas and Judas? It is moments like these that we must take a break from the world of apologetics and enter back into the world of theology.

Unlike many other religious books, the Bible is not a personalized self-help guide that descended from the heavenly places. It is one story told through the eyes of a people chosen by God in a particular place in history, in a particular culture. Every story is true, every command valid, and every law has value. But none of these things can be removed from their original context. What the skeptic seems to miss is one of the foundational principles of the study of biblical interpretation: the Bible can never mean what it never meant. So what might seem like a contradiction, or irregularity, or inaccurate recording of an event can simply be resolved by a clear understanding of the context. When we know why a particular part of Scripture was written, the culture in which it was written, and the people it was originally written to, the vastness of the gospel message comes to life in a much more meaningful way.

CONCLUSION

Whether people admit it or not, every belief needs to have its foundation in some source, in other words, a reason to believe its claims or assertions. The difference between Christianity and every other religion is that the claims of Christianity are grounded in historical fact. Through biblical and non-biblical scholarship we can show the historical reliability of the New Testament Scriptures. This will provide the apologist a basis for the claims regarding Jesus and God's program for redeeming creation from the slavery of sin, forcing our audience to pay attention to the biblical storyline.

CONVERSATION STARTER

I continue to tell students that I think the evidence for the New Testament is one of the most compelling evidence for Christianity. Ask them to consider the consequences of trusting the New Testament from it being a historically accurate document as well as spiritually authoritative.

How would respond to those who argue that the Bible is nothing more than mythical tales with no historical value or credibility?

CHAPTER FOURTEEN
IS THE NEW TESTAMENT AUTHORITATIVE?

Several years ago I had a student named Mary. She was a tremendous student. Articulate, intelligent, loved her classmates, and had an insatiable love for Christ. Yet her and I never seemed to see eye to eye. I did not doubt that her love for Christ and fellow students was genuine, but every time I taught on various topics of the Bible that concerned morality or other sinful behaviors she would object. After several weeks of locking horns with Mary, I decided to meet with her father. We spoke for over an hour and what I learned opened my eyes in a way I had not expected. Mary loved Jesus but had no intention of following him.

Mary liked the idea of Jesus and deeply desired to treat people right, but for her, that meant picking and choosing what she wanted from the Bible. She decided which parts of Scripture held authority in her life and she decided what parts should be taken seriously. For her loving one's neighbor was serious business, but illicit sexual behaviors condemned in Scripture were outdated and irrelevant. Mary believed that to think otherwise was to be hateful. So anytime I taught on what it meant to follow Jesus, or on the idea of objective morality, Mary would either tune out or turn several dark shades of red. Mary could not follow Jesus completely because she didn't view Scripture rightly.

So far we have seen that the New Testament documents are reliable. They are well-researched, historical documents that give credence to the accounts of the disciples and the claims of Jesus. But the Bible is not just some history book. According to the Christian worldview, it is a book (or collection of books) unlike any other. It is the inspired Word of God. If I am simply attempting to add value to the biblical and historical accounts of Jesus and his disciples, then the inspired nature of Scripture does not hold the greatest importance. If I, however, am working to show how Christians should use the Bible—how to interact with others, live out their faith, what it means to follow Jesus, etc.—then two specific challenges arise that need to be addressed so we (and our students) don't make the same mistake Mary did.

The first challenge is the wide range of views regarding the authority Scripture has on the life of a believer. Is Scripture the final authority on all aspects of Christian life, or is much of the Bible simply a suggestion based on the lives of people in a culture far different from our western world? The second challenge is how one views the inspiration of Scripture. Is the Bible completely error free and written by men under the direction of the Holy Spirit or a well-written book by godly men, yet still prone to error? Even among fellow Christians, we must be clear about the nature of Scripture and what it means in the life of a follower of Christ.

Below is a general overview of some of the major views concerning these two areas, as well as a short review of what Scripture teaches regarding how we view and use the Word of God.

MAINSTREAM VIEWS OF AUTHORITY

Most would assume that the authority of God would hold as the supreme norm for all that Christians consider being true. However, the way this authority is expressed varies widely among Christian circles. This muddies the water, even more, when it comes to apologetic arguments. So to understand and maintain a proper view and understanding of God, we must first consider all mainstream views. This way, as we engage others regarding worldviews, we are prepared to answer questions about the nature of the Bible and the authority on which the Christian worldview is built.

Liberalism: A product of the Age of Enlightenment, liberalism focuses on the individual's rights and liberties, freeing people from the confines of ultimate authority. However, the absence of an objective standard or authority, whether government or otherwise, leads to a severe form of subjectivism that "stands as the hallmark of liberalism, though the focus of their subjectivism may vary with different people. So one person could say, 'The Word of God includes any act of God by which communication occurs between God and man.' That communication comes through human reason, feelings, or conscience."[96]

When we talk about subjectivism, we are asserting that one's view is solely based on feeling or personal taste and is dependent on that person's existence, experience and reason. Subsequently, Liberalism has made human reason the judge of truth and often the creator of it. Therefore, higher authority for truth is eliminated. Two specific issues arise from this way of thinking.

The first issue is the finite nature of the human mind. We simply cannot rely on our capacity to make judgments based on what we feel like because our feelings are never constant. Second is our sinful nature. If we take the Bible to be correct, then the human condition stands totally depraved and therefore lacks the ability to define what is right and wrong without some greater authority.

So what happens when we judge authority essentially on the basis of mood? We create a religious experience that emphasizes feelings and awareness of self rather than God. We get a brand of theology attempting to reconcile the rise of the Enlightenment ideology and Protestant theology with Romanticism. In order to marry the mind of science and theology with the heart of emotion, one theologian, Friedrich Schleiermacher (1768-1834), the Father of Modern Liberal Theology, created an updated version of biblical interpretation. However, he ended up creating a theology that became more anthropology and psychology than theology. In other words, creating a theology that is focused on man and his behaviors rather than focused on God.

This attitude could have a significant impact on our theology, giving a person only a partial worship experience—a highly romanticized version of worship which becomes much more imaginative and idealistic, rather than practical—a religion focused on man rather than God. Further, our knowledge is unreliable and limited, so when the basic moral instincts of the human soul become the basis for authority, we are setting the stage for moral relativism.

In all forms of liberalism, human nature is the source of religious truth. Consequently, the Bible becomes the product of human reason containing man's views, thoughts, and feelings about God, rather than God's Word. Essentially the divine inspiration of the Bible is eliminated, thus removing the credibility of the New Testament documents we established in the last chapter.

Conservatism: Contrary to liberalism, conservatives find the basis of authority to be external to man and found only in God. This could be through the church, Scripture, or a combination of both. On the one hand, Conservative Catholicism finds sole authority in the church, which is ordained by the ultimate authority, God Himself. But if man is the one who operates the daily activities of the church, then does this suggest that the church is vulnerable to the same subjectivism liberals face?

On the other hand, the Reformed movement asserts what is known as, *Sola Scriptura;* authority resides in the Scriptures alone. The Scriptures contain the objective revelation of God and are therefore the basis of authority. It would seem as though the typical Protestant church hold to this view in everything concerning Christian faith and life. But is this the case? Is it possible to use only an ancient text as a guide for life in the twenty-first century?

Using Scripture alone would also suggest that God no longer chooses to reveal Himself outside the confines of the Bible. If so, what is bound to happen to our view of the Bible and Christianity? Many Protestant groups deny that the Bible is the sole authority and assert that God can and has revealed Himself in ways that break the confines of the biblical text but do not contradict the biblical text.

Neo-Orthodoxy (Neo = new, Ortho = right/correct, doxy = teaching/instruction): In an effort to address how God can reveal Himself and therefore where the authority of God resides, Neo-Orthodoxy attempts to bridge the gap between liberals and conservatives. Neo-Orthodoxy is different than Liberalism which insists that God, not man must initiate revelation, but it is not conservative, as their view of the Bible still seems to be a liberal view. Karl Barth (1886-1968) believed the basis of authority is the Word, but the Word is Christ. The Bible witnesses to the Word, and does so fallibly, and Christian proclamation is a word about the Word.[97]

Although neo-orthodoxy considers God to be the author and initiator of revelation, the actual reality of one's faith experience is left totally up to the individual. The Bible is indeed involved in these experiences—only man can be allowed to be the judge of them. As a result, there is no room for an external, objective standard of authority. The Bible is then considered fallible and only an instrument with which to encounter Christ. For example, Sally believes in Jesus and reads her Bible. To her, the Bible is a storybook that describes how God had shown himself to the world. Sin for Sally is a function of culture; the Bible merely shows what was sin in the time before and during Jesus' life.

CONCLUSION

Think through each of these views. Which seems to be the best option? Are any of these ideal, or should there be another alternative altogether? My student Mary took something of a Neo-Orthodox view. For her, much of the Bible is irrelevant and outdated but does provide some useful insight as to how the ancient world saw and responded to God—so that we don't fall into their same errors. For my students, Mary was not the only one. Despite the many who raised their hands in worship, professed faith in Christ, attended church regularly, and even prayed with fellow students; many of them failed to live committed lives of following Christ because they refused to recognize the authority of Scripture.

If the Bible is to be considered inspired, it is not only incorrect but also dangerous to assert that man has the sole authority or initiates revelation. We are then allowing the sinful nature of man to define the nature of God and His moral standards. However, man is an important piece, as we are the chosen agents through whom God advances His kingdom plan. If the Bible is inspired by God and the inerrant Word of God, then the divine revelation of God—whether through Scripture, nature, or otherwise—becomes a propositional truth. The Scriptures are independent of me. In other words, the Bible is the Word of God whether I interact with it or not, and God has revealed Himself and stands as the final authority over all of creation, whether I choose to see it or not. The more informed we are of the different ways of viewing Scripture, the more productive our conversations will be.

CONVERSATION STARTER

It is not enough to just see the Bible as a reliable historical record. We also need to recognize its divine authority. Otherwise, we diminish its life-changing power.

How might you help another see the power and importance of seeing the authoritative nature of Scripture correctly?

CHAPTER FIFTEEN

JESUS: MORE THAN A DEAD OLD JEWISH GUY

Let's recap. We can demonstrate the likelihood that God exists. We have seen the need to show that there is a creator of the universe. We have dealt with the problem of evil, its nature, origin, and solution. We understand that the documents which make up the canon of the Bible are reliable, historical documents proved to be at least as, if not more, trustworthy then any other historical documents about the ancient world.

But, for the Christian, all of this evidence boils down to one thing—the resurrection of Jesus. The Apostle Paul made clear that without the resurrection of Jesus, faith in Christ is nothing more than faith in vain and misplaced wishful thinking (1 Cor. 15:14). So to complete the task of creating a cumulative case for the Christian worldview, we can now move to looking into the central claim of the Christian faith. The man Jesus of Nazareth who was born of a virgin, lived a sinless life as the Son of God and God incarnate, was crucified by the Roman government, and resurrected three days after being declared dead and placed into a tomb. If we are correct in asserting that the New Testament documents are a reliable source of historical record, then we must take serious consideration to the claims made about Jesus in those documents.

WHO IS JESUS?

During his earthly ministry two thousand years ago Jesus claimed that he was God. Not just a god, but that he was the Maker of the heavens and the earth and that only through him could mankind experience true peace and be given eternal life. He not only issued this dramatic declaration, but he also had the credentials to back up those claims. This is what separates him from every other major religious figure in history. And what distinguishes orthodox Christianity from its closest rivals like Jehovah's Witnesses, Mormons, and Christian Science. The very uniqueness of Jesus is his claim to deity.

But even in the first-century world of Jesus there was significant confusion over who Jesus was. The role of the Messiah, what the general population thought versus what the Pharisees were afraid of, and what the disciples knew to be true seemed to all be up for debate.

> When Jesus came to the region of Caesarea Philippi, he asked his disciples, "Who do people say the Son of Man is?"..."But what about you?" he asked. "Who do you say I am?" Matthew 16:13, 15

There is no other person in history better known than Jesus of Nazareth. There is no person in history that made the claims he made and did the things he did. Therefore, I think it is safe to assume that the majority of the American population has at least heard of Jesus, maybe has even seen a picture of him hanging in the hallway of a church they once visited. However, although it may seem like almost everyone has at least heard of who Jesus is, the fact of the matter is that even some Christians have an incomplete or even misinformed picture of Jesus. Many in the western world have opted for the teachings of Jesus as if he was some kind of religious sage with some great ideas about life and morality, but neglect the meaning of his sacrifice and the scope of salvation found in the gospel.

Discussing Christianity without confronting the reality of Jesus is impossible. He did not leave us that option. On the pages of the gospels we are forced to do something with his virgin birth, miracles, forgiving of sins, worldview, teaching, death, and ultimately his resurrection. Jesus leaves us no room to reduce him to simply a good moral teacher or religious sage of some sort who ticked off the Jewish religious institution of the first-century and was crucified as a result.

UNDERSTANDING JESUS

Despite the efforts of biblical scholars, church pastors, and teachers to keep Jesus in his historical-cultural context, it seems almost like an American pastime to make Jesus something popular and culturally relevant. Each culture and generation tends to portray a version of Jesus to make him relevant to his or her particular culture, social structures, economic infrastructure, etc. Our western culture, in particular, has created a Jesus that resembles everything from the good old American boy, the hippie of the 1960's, or a hyper-masculine version in the likes of Rocky Balboa or John Wayne. He has even resembled the comforting and compassionate female, somehow ignoring the reality that Jesus was a first-century Jewish Rabbi and son of a carpenter from a little poor, no name town in Israel.

Making Jesus culturally relevant is an attempt to identify with who Jesus is in hopes to make him more relevant to our twenty-first century world. But in the process, avoids the reality of Jesus' character and mission. It is an attempt to enjoy the salvation without the sacrifice. Our job in apologetics is to paint the picture of the real Jesus, the one who was the Jewish Messiah, the God-man, and the savior of the world. Jesus does not need us—or our churches—to make him relevant. His credibility stands on its own.

Beyond the popularity of Jesus in our various intimate social structures is the attention Jesus receives from other religions and cults. The Jehovah's Witnesses view Jesus as the angel Michael. Mormons consider Jesus to be one of many gods. The new age guru and doctor, Deepak Chopra, states that Jesus is a good teacher with many things to say that we can all learn from, but he is not the only way to God. Islam sees Jesus as just another prophet, the prequel to Muhammad. Finally, Hindus see him as most likely one who achieved a high level of reincarnation similar to the Krishna.

Each of these groups clearly understands the importance of dealing with the credibility and claims of Jesus of Nazareth. Yet because of previous religious belief systems, social structure, and other influences, they fail to see the complete picture—a picture illustrating Jesus as the one true way to God the Father, the only way to salvation and into the kingdom of God. Even among Christians, there is some disagreement and confusion as to how we ought to view Christ.

Some see Jesus as one who sits as the ultimate standard and the unachievable perfection of humanity. The focus is set on the "rules" rather than Christ, the law, rather than the lawgiver. While obedience certainly is important, an overzealous focus can lead to a Jesus who is cold and distant and a religion centered on legalism. The result could be a repeat of the Jewish Pharisaic world Jesus came to disrupt. For others, Jesus is full of love, grace, mercy, and tolerance as well as being our King who rules over all people and wishes to extend His kind hand over all. Jesus is the most politically correct person ever to walk the earth. Jesus' chief responsibility is his social obligation and duty to justice. Finally, Jesus is portrayed as someone who comes alongside them as a personal assistant to help achieve specific goals. The appeal of this Jesus is that he is seen as the greatest self-help coach and motivational speaker in the history of the world, rather than the Creator of all that exists.

These views of Jesus are not wrong per se, but the problem is that they are incomplete. The Jesus we need to know, study, follow and help others follow is each of these, in part. "Jesus came to the earth to reveal himself to us as our prophet who speaks to us, priest who walks with us and the king who rules over us."[98] They are incomplete independent of each other, but when we take a little of each, we see that Jesus is a prophet, a priest, and king. As a prophet, he is one who brings a message directly from the Father—a message of grace, redemption, peace and an exodus from our condition of slavery. As a priest, he is the one who intercedes to the Father on our behalf. Though we are a people tainted by sin and unable to approach the throne of grace, Jesus has made it possible. Finally, Jesus as the king portrays the supremacy of Jesus over the entire scope of creation, now in the present creation and in the future in the new creation.

However, what each of these views has in common is the undeniable assertion that Jesus is God. The notion of Jesus as Messiah is simply an assertion that Jesus is from God. Many Jewish revolutionaries before Jesus claimed to be the Messiah—to be anointed by God. However, asserting Jesus is God is a much bolder and serious claim. Additionally, Jesus claims that he is the *only* way to God. Jesus said, "I am the way, the truth, and the life. Nobody gets to the Father but by me" (John 14:6). This bold claim forces the listener or reader to a choice. How you choose to respond and what you choose to make of Jesus Christ is the most important decision you will ever make.

MORE THAN JUST A GOOD MORAL TEACHER

According to Jesus, to know God and know His mission, we must know and accept Jesus. Throughout Scripture, there is an undeniable connection between Jesus and God the Father. A simple survey of the gospels would reveal very clearly that access to the kingdom is only through Jesus because the kingdom belongs to Jesus. Consequently, the mission of God is accomplished through Jesus.

If Jesus is deemed the one who will bring about the kingdom, the one who will bring redemption, freedom, and a life in community with the Creator, then he must be identified with God in some way. Furthermore, if Jesus is deemed to be the one to accomplish the very acts of God, then, in order for Jesus to carry out such a task, in order for him to perform the necessary tasks leading the people of God into a second exodus, Jesus needs to not only be identified with God, but identified as God.

The New Testament is littered with passage after passage, which leads us to an understanding of Jesus as God himself. He forgave sin, he performed miracles, he accepted the title of being *good*, he never sinned, he claimed to be the only way to heaven, he spoke of his resurrection; he accepted worship, he taught people to pray in his name, and he identified himself as "I AM." There is little doubt that Jesus was far different than most of his Jewish contemporaries might have expected. To be a miracle worker was not completely uncommon in the first-century Jewish world. The claim to be the long-awaited Jewish Messiah was even fairly common. But to say the things Jesus said and to do the things Jesus did set him on an entirely different level. Two specific examples illustrate this beautifully.

First, in Mark chapter 2, Jesus arrives at a house in Capernaum. The crowd is so large people are wall-to-wall inside and crowded all around outside. A paralyzed man, carried by his friends is so desperate to get in front of this great rabbi, the friends get him on the roof where they cut a hole and lower him down. Impressed with the faith of these men, Jesus heals the paralytic, but not before Jesus says something that must have been staggering to the crowd looking on: "Son, your sins are forgiven" (Mark 2:5). This is no ordinary comment. This is not the type of comment any Jewish rabbi, miracle worker, or would-be messiah would make. Mark only records the reaction of the teachers of the Law, but I am sure that many in the crowd shared in their confusion. "Why does this fellow talk like that? He's blaspheming! Who can forgive sins but God alone" (Mark 2:7)? Forgiveness of sins is a job reserved for God and God alone. To imply that you can do the same is nothing short of claiming to be God. The implication here is simple, Jesus reveals to all within earshot that he is in fact, God.

In the second example, John records for us in his gospel a long conversation between Jesus and several irate Jews. The conversation begins when several teachers of the law bring to Jesus, a woman who has committed adultery, attempting to trap Jesus and looking for ways to accuse him. After this brief interaction, Jesus begins to describe at great length just who he claims to be. First, he calls himself the light of the world, follows it up with the keeper of the truth, and, just to be sure they understand, Jesus enlightens his accusers that they are not children of Abraham as they have previously thought, but children of Satan. If such claims are not enough, Jesus takes it beyond what anyone would have expected.

> "I tell you the truth...before Abraham was born, I am." - John 8:58.

Jesus claimed to be the long-expected Jewish Messiah, claimed to be the true king of Israel and also claimed to be the Creator of the world. The title, "I Am" refers to his equality with the very God who spoke to Moses through the burning bush. Moses asked God to reveal His name, and God replied "I Am Who I Am" (Ex. 3:14). Most scholars agree that Jesus stating that he existed prior to Abraham is proving the preexistence of Christ. However, there is more to this statement. Jesus says, "I am;" a direct correlation to God's response to Moses when asked what God's name is. Therefore, Jesus is making the bold claim to be the same God of the Old Testament, the God of Abraham, Isaac, and Jacob.

This claim of Jesus denotes his absolute eternal existence—it is, in fact, a claim to be Yahweh of the Old Testament. We can see this clearly through their reaction in the next verse. The Jews listening to the words of Jesus accused him of blasphemy and attempted to stone Jesus.

GETTING A H.A.N.D. ON IT

The above examples serve as just a snap shot of Jesus making some very significant claims about his identity and mission. However, his claim to divinity reaches far beyond a couple of unique interactions. Instead, his claims span across the New Testament text in four key areas. Over the years, many scholars have used the simple acronym, H.A.N.D. to provide us with the necessary evidence for Jesus' claims to divinity—Honors, Attributes, Names, and Deeds.[99] In each of these areas, Scripture helps us to understand that Jesus shares each of these with God the Father in the same way and to the same degree.

Honors. The Apostle Paul makes it clear that Jesus is honored as the one who holds our eternal future in his hands, as the one who holds the power over life and death (Romans 11:36; Galatians 1:4-5; Philippians 4:20). These doxologies do not praise Jesus to the exclusion of the Father but includes the giving of external honor and glory to Jesus within the monotheistic practice of ascribing such glory to God.

This ascribing of glory goes much farther than words in Paul's letters. Matthew, in his gospel, makes it clear that God the Father is to be the only proper object of worship. Yet, almost in the same breath, we witness Jesus as the very same object of worship (Matthew 2:2, 11; 8:1; 9:18; 14:33; 15:25; 20:20; 28:9,17). As a result, the worship of Jesus as God has become foundational to the Christian life. "To worship him, if he is not God is idolatry; to withhold worship from him, if he is, is apostasy."[100]

Nowhere is this more evident, than in prayer. Paul calls on believers to pray in the name of Jesus, indicating the divinity of Jesus. As one who calls on the name of the Lord is a regular Old Testament formula for worship and prayer (Genesis 4:26; 13:4; Psalm 105:1), but nowhere is the divine testimony of prayer more evident than in the prayer of Stephen at the threshold of death at the hands of the Jews in Acts chapter 7.

> They continued to stone Stephen while he prayed, "Lord Jesus, receive my spirit!" Then he fell to his knees and cried out with a loud voice, "Lord, do not hold this sin against them!" When he had said this, he died. - Acts 7:59-60

Stephen recognizes that Jesus is object and means of salvation, and therefore recognizes his authority and supremacy as equal to the Father.

Attributes. Humanity has been created in the image of God. So naturally, there are some attributes of humanity that we share with our Creator. Parts of God have rubbed off on us. Jesus was human. So we can naturally assume that Jesus has those same attributes rubbed off. But there is something more unique about Jesus and the attributes he shares with God the Father. Along with the attributes we share with God, there are those attributes that God alone possesses.

The attributes we share with God are known as communicable attributes. These are attributes that God shares in some fashion with humanity. These are things like love, faithfulness, compassion, etc. However, God will possess these attributes to a much greater degree than His creation; humanity still is able to love, to have compassion, etc., even if these attributes are incomplete or imperfect.

Conversely, the attributes that only God can have are things like being all-knowing, all-powerful, and eternal. These are known as incommunicable. So if we are going to say that Jesus is like God in that he shares attributes with God, then he must somehow share both communicable and incommunicable attributes. In other words, Jesus must share the exact imprint of God's being (Hebrews 1:3). This perfect likeness of God the Father in Jesus is illustrated with near perfect clarity in two specific attributes.

First, Jesus was not created at his birth but exists as an uncreated, eternal part of the Trinity. We have already noted that Jesus claimed to exist before even Abraham and that his assertion of "I am" is a suggestion of his divine status. But even the writer of Hebrews stresses and confirms the preexistence of Jesus (Hebrews 1:10-12). He quotes Psalm 102:25-27, taking its original context—attributing creation and sovereignty over it to God—and applying it to Jesus. Therefore not only do we have a preexisting Jesus, but we are also affirming his preexistence in a way that equates him with the Lord God himself as the one who is sovereign over creation. If every created thing owes its existence to the Son, the Son himself cannot be a created being (John 1:3, 10; 1 Corinthians 8:6; Colossians 1:16; Hebrews 1:2, 10-12).

Second, Christ—just as God is—immutable. That is, he is unchanging. For the Jewish people and their theology, a changeless God in the midst of an ever-changing world was central to their worldview. The same holds true for Christians. The promise of God from the beginning to the end is representative of God's immutable character. He is steadfast, unchanging, the foundation, and a rock. All of which is also attributed to Jesus. God's perfect and unchanging promises are fulfilled in Jesus (2 Corinthians 1:20), requiring Jesus to maintain the same immutable character.

Names. The names and designations given to Jesus throughout the New Testament are a clear indication that his authority is bound up with

God the Father. Jesus is referred to as God, Lord, Savior, Immanuel, and the eternal Word (John 1:1, 14; 20:28; Titus 2:13; 2 Peter 1:1, 11; Romans 9:5). The use of Hebrew name for God, YHWH (generally pronounced, Yahweh) is translated as Lord in the New Testament and is then applied to Jesus by the New Testament writers. God the Father is known to be God of gods and Lord of lords. This is the same designation given to the reign of Jesus. Lastly, God is described as the first and last, which also applies to Jesus in Revelation.

Deeds. Of the many deeds of God throughout history, two stand as preeminent: God's act in creation and redemption—both of which Jesus shares with God. The New Testament is clear that as God is the creator of all things, and all of which is done in and through Jesus. He is some kind of subordinate figure or subcontractor for God, but the instrumental cause of creation.[101] But just as Jesus is the initiator of creation; he is the object of creation's redemption. Jesus stands as the fulfillment of God's salvation plans for not just Israel, but the rest of the world as well. He is the instrumental cause by which salvation is put into effect.

CONCLUSION

A thorough examination of the Bible's record of Jesus, his deeds, and the formation of the church paint an undeniably clear picture of a man who not only lived a sinless life, but also grew in stature and wisdom with God and man, and ministered inspiring thousands and challenging the establishment. Jesus was more than just a man accused of making himself into God, pushing the envelope, and getting himself killed. If that is all Jesus was and yet was still crucified, he stands as just another failed messiah, and criminal did away with. Instead of just being a man, Jesus was also God.

Here Jesus, although he is God, he did not exploit the equality with God he already possessed. He took on the very form and nature of humanity, but without ridding himself of his divinity. However, the divine nature of Jesus was veiled by his humanity—choosing not to exercise his divine power for a time for the purpose of his kingdom mission (Philippians 2). The humiliation of the Son of God begins with Jesus becoming man and ends with the most degrading, excruciating, painful death possible in the Greco-Roman world. Jesus underwent his death for the sake of others, living a life we cannot and bearing the punishment we didn't.

If Jesus is deemed the one who will usher in the kingdom and new creation, the one who will bring redemption, freedom and a life in community with the Creator. If Jesus is deemed to be the one to carry out the very acts of God; then in order for Jesus to carry out such a task; in order for him to perform the necessary duties leading the people of God into a second exodus, Jesus needs to not only be identified with God but identified as God. New Testament Scholar N.T. Wright notes,

> "...the loving God, rolling up his sleeves (Is. 52:10) to do in person the job that no one else could do; the creator God, giving new life the God who works through his created world and supremely through his human creatures the faithful God, dwelling in the midst of his people; the stern and tender God relentlessly opposed to all that destroys or

distorts the good creation and especially human beings, but recklessly loving all those in need and distress."[102]

CONVERSATION STARTER

Most people (although certainly not all) now accept Jesus as a historical figure that made a great impact on our world. To many, he is a great moral teacher or some kind of religious sage.

How would you steer a conversation about Jesus as a great teacher to a conversation about Jesus as the divine Son of God?

CHAPTER SIXTEEN

THE RESURRECTION: WHAT ARE THE CHANCES?

It seems, in our twenty-first century world, that no matter your worldview, no matter your religion, or lack of; Jesus has no doubt influenced your world in some way. Yet in a world over-spiritualized by the likes of Oprah, Deepak Chopra, and Eckhart Tolle, embracing uncertainty has become the new means of salvation; and Jesus is reduced to just another ideology to muddy the water and make us all the more certain about our uncertainty. But what if we can be certain? What if what we know for sure separates Jesus from the rest of the pack and the rest of the world's ideologies? What if what we know about Jesus and his alleged resurrection makes the water crystal clear?

To be clear, Jesus was a real man, who died by Roman execution. These are considered historical facts. There are very few scholars, secular or sacred, that deny the existence of the man Jesus of Nazareth. The historical evidence is so much so that it is considered dishonest scholarship to attempt to assert otherwise.[103] But what makes the study of Jesus so interesting for some and so divisive for others is not only that he claimed to be God, but that he claimed to defy death by resurrecting from the dead.

The resurrection of Jesus is the most known and celebrated miracle in the history of the world. For Christians, our very life and hope depend on the resurrection. Without it, the Christian faith is meaningless. There is no doubt from the pages of the Bible that Jesus not only rose from the dead. He even predicted it.

The theme of resurrection is a thread woven throughout the entire Bible. It is the climactic moment of salvation history. From the moment creation suffered from the sin of Adam and Eve, God has given His people a glimpse of a new creation, one resurrected and recreated. First, Jesus' resurrection was prophesied in advance.

> By oppression and judgment, he was taken away.
>   Yet who of his generation protested?
> For he was cut off from the land of the living;
>   for the transgression of my people, he was punished.

> He was assigned a grave with the wicked,
>   and with the rich in his death,
> though he had done no violence,
>   nor was any deceit in his mouth.

> Yet it was the Lord's will to crush him and cause him to suffer,
>   and though the Lord makes his life an offering for sin,
> he will see his offspring and prolong his days,
>   and the will of the Lord will prosper in his hand.

> After he has suffered,
>   he will see the light of life and be satisfied;
> by his knowledge my righteous servant will justify many,
>   and he will bear their iniquities.

Therefore I will give him a portion among the great,
    and he will divide the spoils with the strong,
because he poured out his life unto death,
    and was numbered with the transgressors.
For he bore the sin of many,
    and made intercession for the transgressors. - Isaiah 53:8-12

Second, Jesus predicted his resurrection.

Then some of the Pharisees and teachers of the law said to him, "Teacher, we want to see a sign from you."

He answered, "A wicked and adulterous generation asks for a sign! But none will be given it except the sign of the prophet Jonah. For as Jonah was three days and three nights in the belly of a huge fish, so the Son of Man will be three days and three nights in the heart of the earth. - Matthew 12:38-40

He then began to teach them that the Son of Man must suffer many things and be rejected by the elders, the chief priests and the teachers of the law, and that he must be killed and after three days rise again - Mark 8:31

Because he was teaching his disciples. He said to them, "The Son of Man is going to be delivered into the hands of men. They will kill him, and after three days he will rise." - Mark 9:31

"We are going up to Jerusalem," he said, "and the Son of Man will be delivered over to the chief priests and the teachers of the law. They will condemn him to death and will hand him over to the Gentiles, - Mark 10:33

221

The Jews then responded to him, "What sign can you show us to prove your authority to do all this?" Jesus answered them, "Destroy this temple, and I will raise it again in three days." They replied, "It has taken forty-six years to build this temple, and you are going to raise it in three days?" But the temple he had spoken of was his body. After he was raised from the dead, his disciples recalled what he had said. Then they believed the scripture and the words that Jesus had spoken. - John 2:18-22

The fate of not only the Christian but the entire world hinges on the resurrection of Jesus. If what we know about first-century history fails to provide adequate evidence to support the claim that Jesus rose from the dead, then we remain uncertain and in the dark, continuing to wander, looking for answers. However, if what we know about the resurrection provides for us a high degree of certainty, then belief in the resurrection is justified, and our entire world is turned on its ear. New Testament scholar and historian N.T. Wright noted,

> "The resurrection of Jesus offers itself, to the student of history or science no less than the Christian or theologian, not as an odd event within the world as it is but the utterly characteristic, prototypical, and foundational event within the world as it has begun to be. It is not an absurd event within the old world but the symbol and starting point of a new world."[104]

The preeminent resurrection scholar and Liberty University Professor, Gary Habermas noted that "Jesus' resurrection is an actual example of our eternal life. It is the only miracle that, by its very nature, indicates the reality of the afterlife."[105] Core teachings of the

Christian faith may involve the Virgin birth, the miracles of Jesus, and his fulfillment of biblical prophecy, but the entire fate of what Christians know and believe hinges on the resurrection. The Apostle Paul makes it clear that if Christ has not been resurrected that the Christian faith is empty and useless (1 Corinthians 15). It seems as though that more than just the Christian worldview is in jeopardy without the resurrection. In fact, Paul gives us the feeling that the fate of all of humanity dangles on one little strand, which is the resurrection.

If the biblical accounts can be trusted to, at a minimum, give us accurate information about the events surrounding Jesus' life and death, then we can put those events to the test to determine the best possible explanation. Essentially, these resurrection events should be held to the same degree of scrutiny as any other event in history. And like any good historian, regardless of how fantastic or inconceivable the event, the evidence dictates the direction of our conversation.

Therefore the question boils down to what we know or what we can know and how that data is interpreted. For example, from the agnostic point of view, the evidence may be viewed as meaningless since the only thing we are certain of is uncertainty. Which self-destructs. What data is available to support the agnostic's claim? If there is data to the contrary, then certainly it is worth pursuing. Because even if the agnostic is only certain of their uncertainty, then it stands to reason that they are seeking some form of certainty within their worldview. Therefore, if evidence exists that provides firmer ground to stand on; it seems only logical to give it an honest look. Otherwise, any view that ignores simple, sound, and logical evidence; and continues to live contrary to it, is walking dangerously close to psychosis.

So, what then, can we know about the resurrection of Jesus?

When we are looking at the resurrection, there are three key factors that require explanation: the discovery of the empty tomb, the alleged postmortem appearances of Jesus, and the profound transformation of the early disciples.

THE EVIDENCE SURROUNDING THE BIBLE

It can be said with near absolute certainty among scholars (Christians and non-Christians) that Jesus was in fact crucified under the Roman government sometime around A.D. 30-33. Although there a wide variety of scholarship in this area, there is comprehensive agreement that the historical person of Jesus of Nazareth, traveled first-century Palestine as a Jewish Rabbi, and because of the perceived threat on the Jewish religion and the peace of the Roman Empire, he was crucified. Whether biblical scholars or historians, the investigation of the person of Jesus has resulted in almost unanimous consent—and a crucified Jesus has led to the discovery of an empty tomb.

The discovery of the empty tomb. It would have been a strictly followed custom to ensure the body was properly prepared and placed in a tomb prior to the Sabbath; which began at sundown on Friday. Jesus' body would have been wrapped in nearly one-hundred pounds of spices and linens and placed in a tomb guarded by Roman soldiers, of which even Pilate told them to make the tomb as secure as possible (Matthew 27:65). It is commonly understood and accepted by New Testament supporters and critics that Jesus' burial in the tomb, belonging to Joseph of Arimathea, to be one of the best-established facts about the historical Jesus.[106]

All four gospels and Paul corroborate the known tomb and it's being empty three days following the crucifixion. Further, there are no credible competing stories or theories, leaving little doubt that Jesus was in fact buried in a tomb that was later found to be empty. Even liberal scholar A.T. Robertson agrees that, one of the earliest and best-attested facts about Jesus is the burial.[107] However, within these gospels is something more staggering than just an empty tomb; it is an empty tomb discovered by women.

What may not seem like much of a deal becomes incredibly meaningful when placed in context. In first-century Palestine, if one were trying to fabricate a story, in no way were women considered a trustworthy witness to perpetuate such a story. A women's testimony was not admitted: "on the account of the levity and boldness of their sex."[108] Further, if the disciples were trying to fabricate a story why in the world would the gospel writers choose women to be first on the scene as eyewitnesses? So it is likely that from the biblical text the disciples at least thought Jesus had resurrected and behaved as though it were true.

If the tomb had not been empty, the preaching of the apostles could have, and most likely would have, stopped simply by producing Jesus' dead body. If Jesus was the threat that Rome and the Jews thought he was, it was in their best interest to produce a body and put down any unneeded political and religious unrest. Why else would Pilate want the tomb to be guarded? Further, if Jesus had been killed and buried in a tomb and left there, it would have been extremely likely that the tomb would have been venerated as that of a saint. This custom could explain why the women were at the tomb in the first place—possibly preparing the site for later tribute.

The facts of the empty tomb are so clear that in a debate with Gary Habermas, the well-known atheist philosopher, Antony Flew (who later in life professed belief in God) conceded that the tomb was in fact empty.[109] When all the facts are considered, there is little room for doubt that the historical credibility of Jesus' burial clearly supports an empty tomb.[110]

People really did see Jesus alive after the crucifixion. Given the approximately thirty-year gap between the crucifixion and alleged resurrection, some deviation from the truth is not entirely impossible. However, it is not the gospels that provide us with the earliest account of the resurrection. In 1 Corinthians 15, the Apostle Paul provides what most scholars consider to be what is called a pre-Pauline creedal confession dating back as early as 30 A.D.

> "For what I received I passed on to you as of first importance: that Christ died for our sins according to the Scriptures, that he was buried, that he was raised on the third day according to the Scriptures, and that he appeared to Cephas, and then to the Twelve. After that, he appeared to more than five hundred of the brothers and sisters at the same time, most of whom are still living, though some have fallen asleep. Then he appeared to James, then to all the apostles" - 1 Corinthians 15:3-7

This passage is an early creed that Christians recited as a part of worship long before Paul borrowed it for his letter to the Corinthians; and a critical part of Paul's detailed eyewitness account of the postmortem Jesus. Not only is Paul providing his Corinthian audience the details of and the necessity for the resurrection as followers of Jesus, but he is also providing certainty of the historical event. Paul continues to be, among scholars, the undisputed author of 1 Corinthians. Dated sometime in the A.D. 50's, this information is what was passed along to him from the original disciples after his conversion. These verses do not reflect his thoughts, but an early creed passed down to him. In other words, these verses were a foundational piece of early Christianity—as early as A.D. 30. Even the well-known atheistic New Testament scholar and critic, Gerd Ludeman, confirms that "the discovery of pre-Pauline confessional formulations is one of the great achievements in recent New Testament scholarship."[111] Gary Habermas sheds some additional light on this as well.

> "An increasing number of exceptionally influential scholars have very recently concluded that at least the teaching of the resurrection, and perhaps even the specific formulation of the pre-Pauline creedal tradition in 1 Corinthians 15:3-7, dates to A.D. 30! In other words, there never was a time when the message of Jesus' resurrection was not an integral part of the earliest apostolic proclamation. No less a scholar than James D.G. Dunn even states regarding this crucial text: 'This tradition, we can be entirely confident, was formulated as tradition within months of Jesus' death.'"[112]

This formulation is what N.T. Wright calls "unalterable Christian bedrock,"[113] And it shows us that the affirmation of the resurrection was established a short time after the event and added to the early communities fundamental beliefs. Further, it disproves the resurrection as a much later developed legend. Instead, the witnesses Paul speaks of were alive and available for questioning. Therefore it seems clear that Paul was recording what he received from the earliest eyewitness disciples closest to Jesus. Essentially, Paul's testimony and use of this early creed establishes historically that various individuals and groups of people on different occasions at the absolute least, experienced appearances of Jesus alive after his death.[114]

So to recap, we have historical verification of an empty tomb, recorded eyewitnesses that people at least believed Jesus had resurrected and served as a foundational part of the earliest Christian theology.

The incredible transformation of the disciples. The historical record of the early Christians illustrates a group of people who upon the crucifixion of Jesus, fled for fear of their own lives. That is until they believe he resurrected and appeared to them. The attitude of Christians after they had allegedly witnessed a divine miracle radically changed from being fearful to bold proclaimers of the very thing they had seen and what it meant for humanity. There is no doubt that they believed Jesus had resurrected and willingly endangered themselves and suffered, at times, brutal deaths as a result. They lived, as the first-century Roman historian, Tacitus noted, "enemies of the human race."

Just consider the transformation of Peter from the end of the gospels to Acts. During the crucifixion, Peter denied Jesus and fled the scene. However, Peter sees, first-hand the empty tomb and the risen Christ. It is not long before Peter is standing before thousands preaching the gospel, confronted with Jewish religious authority and threatened. But instead of heeding their commands, Peter stays the course and continues to boldly proclaim the gospel (Acts 4:20). This new attitude of Peter is a far cry from the coward we saw at the crucifixion.

If the resurrection did not happen then, scholars need to derive the reasons for the rapid growth of Christianity across the ancient world. How could disciples of Jesus, who did not understand or even conceive of the idea of a resurrection of one person, who could not stand by the side of Jesus risking their own lives while Rome took his; suddenly braved persecution declaring that Jesus had indeed risen from the dead? The earliest and most consistent message of the early church to today has been grounded in the resurrection of Jesus. Otherwise, his death would have no meaning at all.

If the church was, as some continue to suggest, lying, in an effort to perpetuate a myth to make an ordinary man from Nazareth into divinity; then legally speaking, it would be exponentially more difficult to maintain such a lie, given the rapid spread, mass amounts of writing, and incredible growth of Christian beliefs. The complexities of deception far outweigh ordinary truthful communication.[115] John Warwick Montgomery provides for us practical details of the near impossibility of maintaining deceitful communication. He notes that, "the witness engaged in deception must, as it were, juggle at least three balls simultaneously, while continually estimating his chances of discovery: he must be sure he doesn't say anything that contradicts what his examiner knows (or what he thinks his examiner knows); he must tell a consistent lie (liars must have good memories), and he must take care that nothing he says can be checked against contradictory external data."[116]

NON-CHRISTIAN HISTORICAL EVIDENCE FOR THE RESURRECTION

However, the historical facts of Jesus' life and death are not limited to the Christian story and the Bible. Jewish historians and Roman accounts of the new Christian influence illustrate that, at a minimum, there was a group of people who believed there was a man named Jesus who was the promised Messiah to the Jewish people and was crucified and resurrected three days later.

If Jesus and his followers had the impact on the Roman world that the New Testament suggests they did, then we should be able to see evidence of that affect in the writings of Roman and Jewish historians of that period. Tacitus and Suetonius wrote about the actions of Christians as a result of the resurrection, recognizing that their belief in that fact was strong. The same could be said of the Jewish world.

Tacitus: Cornelius Tacitus was a Roman historian who lived through the reign of several emperors and has been called the greatest historian of the ancient Roman world. He is best known for two of his works, *Annals*, and *Histories*. In his Annals, Tacitus mentions Jesus once as he wrote on the burning of Rome during the reign of Nero.

> "But not all the relief that could come from man, not all the Bounties that the prince could bestow, nor all the atonements Which could be presented to the gods, availed to relieve Nero From the infamy of being believed to have ordered the Conflagration, the fire of Rome. Hence to suppress the rumor, he Falsely charged with the guilt and punished Christians, who were hated for their enormities. Christus, the founder of the name, was Put to death by Pontius Pilate, procurator of Judea in

the reign Of Tiberius: but the pernicious superstition, repressed for a time Broke out again, not only through Judea, where the mischief Originated but through the city of Rome also, where all things Hideous and shameful from every part of the world find their Center and become popular. Accordingly, an arrest was first Made of all who pleaded guilty; then, upon their information, an Immense multitude was convicted, not so much of the crime of Firing the city, as of hatred against mankind."[117]

Suetonius: Although disputed, Suetonius (historian and chief secretary to Emperor Hadrian A.D. 117-138) makes what could be interpreted as a reference to Jesus and Christians. Writing about the wave of riots, which broke out in a large Jewish community in Rome in A.D. 49[118], Suetonius wrote,

"Because the Jews at Rome cased continuous disturbances at the instigation of Chrestus, he expelled then from the city."

"Chrestus" is believed by many to be a variant spelling of Christ. Suetonius' second reference refers to Christians who were tortured by Emperor Nero.

"After the great fire at Rome...Punishments were also inflicted on the Christians, a sect professing a new and mischievous religious belief."[119]

Josephus: A Jewish historian born into a wealthy priestly family around the time of Jesus' death served as a Pharisee and later became the court historian for Emperor Vespasian after the destruction of Jerusalem in A.D. 70. His most famous work, *Antiquities*, provides some of the most detailed examples of Jesus and the early Christians.

> "Having such a character, Ananus thought that with Feasts dead and Albinus still on the way he would have the proper opportunity. Convening the judges of the Sanhedrin, he brought before them the brother of Jesus who was called the Christ, whose name was James, and certain others. He accused them of having transgressed the law and delivered them up to be stoned."[120]

IT'S DECISION TIME!

> "I am trying here to prevent anyone saying the foolish thing that people often say about Him: 'I am ready to accept Jesus as a great moral teacher, but I don't accept His claim to be God.' That is the one thing we must not say. A man who is merely a man and said the sort of things Jesus said would not be a great moral teacher, He would either be a lunatic, on the level with a man who says he is a poached egg, or else He would be the devil of Hell. You must make your choice. Either this man was and is the Son of God or else a madman or something worse. You can shut Him up for a fool, you can spit at Him and kill Him as a demon, or you can fall at His feet and call Him Lord and God. But let us not come with any patronizing nonsense about His being a great human teacher. He has not left that open to us. He did not intend to."[121] – C.S. Lewis in Mere Christianity

Just as Lewis aptly points out, we must get off the fence. In our conversations, we must be willing to help people make a decision. The person and work of Jesus is too important, too vital a moment in human history to ignore. We absolutely must come to terms with these pieces of evidence and deal with the results.

The claims leave us with four possible results: Jesus was a legend, a liar, a lunatic, or he was Lord. If Jesus never made the claim to be God, then this whole Jesus thing is simply a legend. However, based on the reliability of the New Testament documents, we can clearly assert he made the claim. If Jesus did, in fact, make the claim to be God, but the claim was false, and he knew it, it makes him a liar. On the other hand, if Jesus did not know the claim was false, then he is reduced to a lunatic. Finally, if Jesus made the claim and the claim is true, then there is nothing left to do but declare Jesus as Lord.

CONCLUSION

Theologically, the resurrection holds supreme importance as it reveals the identity of Jesus as not just the God-man who brought freedom from sin, but as the beginning of a future age. What God was going to do for Israel and the world, he was beginning to do through Jesus, Israel's Messiah, the Son of God.[122] In other words, the resurrection constitutes the dawning of the new creation (Romans 8:18-22). However, the impact of the resurrection reaches far beyond the theological circles of Christians and their churches.

According to philosopher William Lane Craig, three-quarters of scholars who have written on the subject accept the fact of the empty tomb; virtually no one denies that the earliest disciples experienced post-mortem appearances of Jesus; and far and away, most scholars agree that the earliest disciples at least believed that God had raised Jesus from the dead.[123] Therefore, the overwhelming evidence eliminates the possibility of any alternative explanations and continually directs the honest seeker back to the resurrection. If Jesus resurrected, then he is certainly worth paying attention to. If Jesus resurrected, then we can logically conclude that God does in fact exist. If Jesus resurrected, then we can logically conclude that the theological impact of the resurrection will have a direct impact on all creation, not just a select few.

In any conversation about Jesus, we cannot allow people to escape the reality of Jesus by agreeing to his "good moral teaching." We must, with great gentleness and respect, show people the edge of the proverbial cliff. Their views of Jesus will ether push them off the cliff, or talk them off the edge, but they must pick which one. Therefore, we must also show them the implication of each. Accepting Jesus is more than just a heartfelt realization and confession of one's sin. It is a call of self-denial and sacrifice.

While there will always be parts of our lives that remain uncertain, the historical reliability of the resurrection of Jesus Christ provides clarity of the condition of our world now and the certainty of hope of the world to come. The resurrection of Jesus "ushers in not simply a new religious possibility, not simply a new ethic or a new way of salvation, but a new creation."[124]

CONVERSATION STARTER

Just like our conversation about the existence of God, there will always be a wide range of debates regarding the resurrection of Jesus. Below are a few of the most common objections. Discuss with your students how you might overcome them.

The disciples faked the resurrection.

The resurrection was a myth later created by the church to deify Jesus.

The disciples were so traumatized by the crucifixion that they hallucinated and just thought they saw a resurrected Jesus

CHAPTER SEVENTEEN
CONVERSATIONS: YUP...YOU HAVE TO TALK TO PEOPLE

I was doing the dishes after dinner one evening when there was a knock on the door. Standing on my front porch were two young Mormon missionaries eager to talk to me. I paused for a second to let my family know I would be outside for a few minutes. I stepped out onto the porch with them and talked with them for over an hour. We made small talk for a few minutes, but it didn't take us long to dive in. We talked about the Book of Mormon, the Bible, and of course, the nature of Jesus. They were as insistent on their points as I was on mine. As we wrapped up the conversation, they continued to be confident in the authority of the Book of Mormon but left with plenty of questions to consider. They didn't convert to Christianity or say a sinner's prayer. But I was happy with the conversation. Why? Because my goal was not to convert; it was to establish a positive relationship, provide the necessary evidence, and create some discord in their minds about what they believed—and to do all of this without being a terrible jerk.

Yes, after all of this learning, the final item on our list is actually making an effort to talk to people. Now for some of you, the thought of going beyond book learning to faith sharing makes being beaten and burned look like the better option. But at the same time, we know that Jesus said otherwise.

> Go therefore and make disciples of all the nations, bap-tizing them in the name of the Father and the Son and the Holy Spirit, teaching them to observe all that I commanded you; and lo, I am with you always, even to the end of the age." – Matthew 28:19-20

> But you will receive power when the Holy Spirit comes on you, and you will be my witnesses in Jerusalem, and in all Judea and Samaria, and to the ends of the earth." – Acts 1:8

But there is good news. Just like my conversation with the two Mormon missionaries, you don't have to feel the pressure to convince everyone you meet. Don't force the conversation. Discussions about spiritual things often come naturally, just be listening for it. Be proactive. Seek out the opposing worldview, find the flaws and make your case for the Christian worldview.

APOLOGETICS IS ABSOLUTELY NEEDED

Consider once again the actions and lifestyle of Jesus. As discussed earlier, Mark 2 illustrates Jesus' claim to be the Son of Man, and the Creator God made known through his actions to the paralytic and His comments to the Pharisees. "Which is easier to say?" Both are equally easy to make. But where is the proof? Looking at the miracles of Jesus, there is always some greater truth attached. In this passage as well as others, it is his identity. Jesus himself sets the stage for the justification of Christian apologetics by creating a Philosophy of Demonstration among his followers.

Continuing after Jesus, the apostles encouraged believers to defend the faith (1 Peter 3:14-16), contend for the faith (Jude 3), and to refute, not repress it (Titus 1:9). Further, the apostles and gospel writers modeled apologetic activities (Luke 1). Finally, Paul reasons, proving and persuading on behalf of the truth of the gospel (Acts 17), to those who are biblically illiterate by using the biblical plotline to provide a proper frame of reference that goes back to Genesis. Paul points to the resurrection as the reason that Jesus is the proper object of faith. Faith in Christ is grounded in the hope of a future resurrection. However, this hope in Christ stems from a promise given by God to Abraham in Genesis. Jesus then becomes the proof of God's covenant faithfulness to the nation of Israel and consequently all nations (Genesis 12). Our hope in Christ becomes grounded in the faithful promises of God and is, therefore, reasonable to believe.

As ambassadors of Christ, we cannot think for one moment that we are absolved from our responsibility of defending the gospel. It should be a part of who we are in Christ, and we should treat defending the gospel the same as we would proclaiming the gospel. In Acts, defense and proclamation, in many cases, went hand in hand. This not only provided a means by which to spread the gospel but also provided an avenue to strengthen believers' faith.

A careful reading of Acts 26 shows that Paul's defense to King Agrippa is woven within his experience of the risen Lord. All that

Paul has experienced has taught him what is true and reasonable, not only regarding emotion but regarding knowledge. There is an unmistakable connection between the discipleship of the mind and genuine or authentic worship (Romans 12), and therefore a connection between the mind and spiritual growth (2 Cor. 10:3-5).

We cannot continue to believe that our nation and culture is immune to spiritual warfare. In fact, western civilization, is for the first time in history, in danger of dying. Apologetics is meant not to save the church but to save the world. We are not only in a civil and cultural crisis, but also in a philosophical and intellectual crisis. The idea of objective truth is being attacked, especially by education and the rest of the public square. At the deepest level, this crisis is not cultural or intellectual; it is spiritual. The eternal souls for whom Christ died are at stake.

USING THE WORLDVIEW QUESTIONS

Now that you have studied the evidence for Christianity, the truth claims that surround it and the fact that Christianity is buried in reality, you can begin to engage in confident conversation with anyone and everyone. When speaking with my new Mormon friends, I didn't focus on making my case right out of the gate. I began the conversation by asking questions. I asked what they thought about Jesus, salvation, and the nature of the church—all without making any assumptions about what Mormon's believe in general. I wasn't interested in what Mormons believe. I was interested in what they believed. Even as we dove deeper, I continue directing the questions. I showed them passages from John on the divinity of Jesus and asked for their thoughts. They introduced me to several passages in the Book of Mormon, and I asked how they knew those passages to be true. We disagreed on many ideas, challenged each other, and yet always respected each other.

So make your first step to find out what the other person's worldview is, by building relationships. The easiest method is to begin by asking the worldview questions presented in chapter three. You could do this in a formal sense, by asking the person to sit with you and answer each question in sequence. However, the likelihood of sitting down to a formal conversation each time is not all that realistic. Therefore, I suggest using the questions as starting points for informal conversations that happen throughout the day. Keep in your back pocket, questions like, "what do you mean by that?" and "how did you come to that conclusion?" Be willing to fail, and willing to practice. Either way, finding out their worldview determines how they see the world and will determine how you approach your conversation.

Once you have an idea of their worldview, you can begin to find common ground. The more questions you ask, the more common ground you are likely to find. Find some areas of truth you can agree on. Do not be afraid to agree with them. For example, you could agree that some higher power exists, that many Christians are hypocrites, or there is too much evil in the world. This establishes a relationship and assures the person you are not just waiting to shove the gospel at them the first chance you get. Be patient and let the Spirit guide you.

When the opportunity presents itself, ask if they would like to hear your thoughts on the matter. Or you can ask questions in such a manner that the Christian alternative to their view manifests itself with little to no effort. However, do not expect to be great at this immediately. This takes practice, time, and patience. In some cases, you may have several conversations with a person over several months, even years, before much ground is gained.

Try to ask all five questions during the course of a conversation. Ask plenty of follow up questions. Spend the time probing about why he thinks and believes what he does and where he received his information about his worldview. Look for holes in his thinking. These are opportunities to present your thoughts. Just be sure to offer your opinion, not asserting it as fact—the facts speak for themselves. Above all, have fun witnessing the Spirit of God move through you to bring another into the kingdom.

CONCLUSION

Now that you have completed this book, please do not let the skills and methods you have learned simply pass away. Use them. A lot. The more you work to intentionally engage people in worldview discussions, the more you will find yourself doing the work of an apologist. The easier and more natural it will become.

Whether you choose to use the worldview interview questions in a formal sense or simply as a guide in conversation, understanding a person's worldview is essential in creating productive, meaningful interaction with non-Christians. Additionally, knowing how Christianity makes sense builds us into confident, bold, people of God who proclaim the risen Jesus.

As you step out and go make disciples, remember two things. First, for some people, they may never read a Bible or step into a church, so you may be the only Jesus they ever see. Second, each of us has been called to represent the risen Christ here on earth and demonstrate what the gospel looks like in action.

CONVERSATION STARTER

Now go...and start a conversation. Begin a new relationship and a new opportunity to move the gospel forward.

APPENDIX A

HOW TO MAKE APOLOGETICS PART OF YOUTH MINISTRY DNA

It starts with integrating the practice of apologetics into your youth ministry. But how? There are few key ways that with very little effort you can expose students to other worldviews, arguments, and objections to Christianity in a controlled environment grounded in biblical truth.

CREATE A CULTURE OF QUESTIONS

Students have questions. There is no way around it, and there is no way of avoiding it. Nor should you. So it is critical that you can foster a culture where questions are encouraged. But don't freak out just yet. I am *not* saying that you must have all the answers to every question every student asks. Believe me; they will devise some kind of crazy question that you can't answer—or even should answer. That isn't the point. The point here is to make certain that students feel safe to ask and wrestle with huge questions.

Although it might be hard to imagine, there are many students who have been raised to believe that to doubt and question is to have insufficient faith. Think about John the Baptist for a moment. He sat in jail wondering if Jesus really was the Messiah, or had he made a mistake? So did he have insufficient faith? The key here is to look at the response Jesus gives to John's disciples to be delivered back to John. He does not rebuke, express disappointment, or laugh in their faces. Jesus simply responded with evidence.

> "So he replied to the messengers, "Go back and report to John what you have seen and heard: The blind receive sight, the lame walk, those who have leprosy are cleansed, the deaf hear, the dead are raised, and the good news is proclaimed to the poor. Blessed is anyone who does not stumble on account of me." - Luke 7:22-23

Jesus rattles off several pieces of evidence that, in Jesus, the kingdom was coming indeed. He essentially gave John exactly what he needed to hear. Questions and doubts can be incredibly productive when it leads to answers and certainty. Create a culture that encourages students to ask the tough questions and then explore answers together.

PUT STUDENTS IN THE HOT SEAT

Creating the right culture is a great start, but students need to experience real life conditions. When soldiers go into boot camp, they don't merely sit inside a classroom asking their commander questions. Instead, the vast majority of their training is experiencing battle-like conditions in a simulated environment. I often think of high school ministry the same way, by giving students simulated experiences based on what they will encounter in the world beyond the safety of their Christian world.

I call it the *Hot Seat*. What usually started off, as terrifying for some students quickly became one of the most popular days in many of my classes as a teacher. And surprisingly it works just as well in a youth group setting. Essentially this is a role-playing exercise designed to engage other worldviews. You can do this in two ways.

First, bring in a stranger. Have them play the role of another worldview and present their case to your students. Make sure they are well educated and can answer a few objections. Let the students ask the questions after the presentation. Be sure to spend time debriefing with your students. This is where some of the best lessons are learned. Think about everything with them. From what they heard in the presentation, what sounded good to what was inconsistent. How did they respond? How should they have responded? This is also a good time to teach love and respect when speaking with a person of a different worldview.

Second, change this scenario up a little by doing a one-on-one. I usually did this on stage with either two students—one playing the role of Christian and the other another worldview. Or I would ask for a student volunteer to ask me a series of questions, and I would play the role of another worldview. For this one, you will want a predetermined series of questions and a confident student. However, this option is not necessarily designed to benefit the student volunteer. It is designed to instruct the rest of the group. Be sure to get them involved. Again, debrief. Think about both sides of the argument and the demeanor of each. If necessary, stop in the middle of the exercise to teach or redirect.

But I cannot stress this enough. You must spend time debriefing with students. Only do what *your* students are ready for and be ready for questions, comments, and concerns. Remember, it is better to expose students to other worldviews in a controlled environment to better prepare them for the real deal.

CALL IN THE EXPERTS

Have you ever heard of the 50-mile rule? A friend and former colleague of mine introduced me to this a number of years ago. Think of it this way: You have a group of students that you are speaking to, mentoring, etc. and provide them with some amazing truths from Scripture. Its reception is only lukewarm. But some time later, maybe at a retreat or conference, another speaker who traveled in from another state or part of the country says the same thing and the students act like they have never heard it before and the truth blows their minds. This is the 50-mile rule. The further away a person lives, the more authority they seem to have. Sometimes if you want to drive home a point in the hearts and minds of your students, you have to bring in a guest speaker. One who is not local and who has some authority on the subject.

This does a couple of key things for you as a youth leader. First, it takes the pressure off of you. If apologetics is not your thing and you don't feel confident in discussing it at great length and depth with your students, then you will naturally shy away from it. Unless of course, you decide to read a dozen books on the subject. But truthfully, who has time for that? Second, it can reinforce what you have been teaching. It was like when we were kids. If mom tells us something we would rather not believe, then we ask dad. If we still refuse to believe it, then we ask our friend's mom. Or better yet, a celebrity reinforces what mom was saying all along. Only then do we concede.

However, don't just go for the most popular speaker money can buy. Take some time to figure out what your students need. What questions do they have? What are they most struggling with? What kind of speaker do they need? There are a huge variety of topics, backgrounds, and styles available. Be aware of what and who your students will respond to.

USE CURRICULUM AND ELIMINATE THE GUESS WORK

Finally, if you are looking to dive much deeper into apologetics then I would suggest committing an entire year to the task. I would take a systematic approach and consider investing in some quality curriculum that will help you guide your students through some difficult concepts. Apologetics is not an easy study and not a topic to be taken lightly. Using a well-organized curriculum can be a huge advantage. Which is precisely why Awana Youth Ministries teamed up with Sean McDowell to create Advocates.

We recognized the incredible void in curriculum designed around youth apologetics yet the deep need to train students to engage their culture with truth in humble dialogue. Advocates provides youth leaders—bi-vocational, full-time, or part-time—with a comprehensive suite of tools that will train students to always be prepared (1 Peter 3:15), take every thought captive (2 Corinthians 10:5), defend the truth with sound doctrine (Jude 3), and speak truth in love (Ephesians 4:15). It is far more than simply worldviews or world religions training; its truth training. It is learning to live the Christian worldview in a world that has categorically rejected it.

Ask yourself how Jennifer's story from the introduction might have turned out had she been prepared for her professor's worldview. When I began this week's blog, I almost 10 different ideas, and am sure I could come up with twenty or more. These are just a few of my favorites. The point is, is that you engage your students in some fashion to apologetic topics, arguments from skeptics, or other worldviews. Create an environment where they can ask questions, make mistakes, raise doubts, and come to conclusions that appropriately reflect biblical truth. We live in a world that is far too dangerous to sit back and do nothing, hoping that a weekly sermon, worship music, and maybe a retreat or two is enough. It's not. Doing nothing is no longer an option.

My challenge to you is this: pick just one of these ideas and run with it. Watch how your students respond. Stick with it, and you'll see seniors graduating with greater confidence and making a greater impact on the world than you imagined they would.

APPENDIX B
WHAT IS GENERATION Z ASKING?

A few nights ago my daughters were watching their favorite cartoon. I am pretty strict on what they watch, and this particular show has been pretty harmless. So I thought. My wife happened to be in the room when this cartoon, written for preschool age children, introduced the concept of two mommies. Taken slightly by surprise, my wife redirected the girls onto another activity. While I am not entirely surprised, this was a great reminder that the world our students are growing up in is far different than yours and mine.

A different world means different questions. Or some of the same questions with vastly different implications. This coming year your youth group will finally be made up of entirely Generation Z. Which means an entirely new set of rules, questions, circumstances, challenges, and future. So as you prepare for this coming fall, be sure that you are ready. Research is beginning to look specifically at how this generation is unique and what questions they are asking. There are many, but here are three of the biggest questions that are helping shape how they see the world and react to it.

HOW CAN I BE SURE?

Every generation possesses a degree of uncertainty. But it seems Generation Z has a particularly hard time. Our world has a much higher degree of uncertainty than generations before. The sheer amount of information available to them is astounding. On the one hand--as I have mentioned before--because of technology and information we have a greater opportunity for knowledge and greater access to the world. Which when it comes to the gospel, equals an opportunity like none other. On the other hand, the more information, the more opinions, and thus the greater chances for confusion.

Students today are looking for certainty. They are looking for assurance. They are looking for mentors that can by guiding them through the mud. They need leaders and parents to clear the water with truth.

WHAT IS MY IDENTITY?

I remember when I was in high school my biggest identity issue was whether I wanted to play football or stay in band. I made a choice, and that became my teenage identity. Sure there were those in my school that through various interactions and circumstances helped shape that identity. But for the most part, we rolled with it. It seemed complicated and treacherous then but now seems so much simpler than what students face today.

Research shows that the majority of identity issues are now focused on issues of sexuality. Not STD's or teen pregnancy, but gender identity. Our politically correct culture has inadvertently taught students that if you are not questioning your gender identity, then perhaps there is something wrong with you. This narrative is causing confusion. It is easy to tell students that their identity rests in Christ, but it is much more powerful, as a leader, to be their example.

WHO CAN I BELIEVE AND TRUST?

Every generation has to grow up in the midst of some sort of change. For some it was war, others it was civil rights, and others, economics or technology. Every generation has its challenges that shape that generation forever. For Generation Z, it just might be all of those lumped into one. This new generation of students is growing in a world of distrust on all kinds of levels with competing narratives and ideology causing violence and arguments worldwide.

So who can students trust? Politicians? Media? Teachers? Parents? Youth leaders and parents need to earn trust through unconditional love and a community that looks like and represents God himself. Students want to feel safe. They want to belong. And they want to be a part of something greater than themselves. In previous generations, the responsibility of role models seemed to belong to athletes, actors, musicians, etc. But research is showing students are returning to their roots for their role models. They are looking for trust within family and close friends. What an incredible challenge that lies before us as youth leaders, but what an amazing opportunity.

This year cannot be youth group as usual. Generation Z is going to change the game. Our students are looking to you to walk with them, do life with them, and help them make sense amid cultural confusion. But most of all, they need you to be the example of Christ and guide to go and make disciples.

END NOTES

[1] Nancy Pearcey, Total Truth: Liberating Christianity Fro Its Cultural Captivity. (Wheaton:

CHAPTER 1

[2] For those not familiar with the Romans Road, it is a method widely used that is designed to walk a person through salvation using Paul's letter to the Romans. The traditional pattern is as follows Romans 3:23, 6:23, 5:8, 10:9, 5:1.

[3] Douglas Groothuis, *Christian Apologetics: A Comprehensive Case For Biblical Faith*. (Downers Grove: InterVarsity Press, 2011), 24.

[4] Definition was taken from www.dictionary.reference.com.

[5] James Taylor, *Introducing Apologetics: Cultivating Christian Commitment* (Grand Rapids, Baker: 2006), 18.

[6] Craig J. Hazen. "Defending the Defense of the Faith" in *Everyone an Answer*. Ed. Francis Beckwith, William Lane Craig and J.P. Moreland. (Downers Grove, InterVarsity Press: 2004), 38.

[7] For further study on this matter see J.P. Moreland. *Love Your God With All Your Mind: The Role of Reason in the Life of the Soul*. (Colorado Springs: NavPress, 1997).

[8] Alister McGrath, *Doubting: Growing Through the Uncertainties of Faith*. (Downers Grove: InterVarsity, 2007),14.

[9] David K. Clark, *Dialogical Apologetics: A Person Centered Approach to Christian Defense* (Grand Rapids: Baker Books, 1993), 114.

[10] Rocky Balboa. Written and Directed by Sylvester Stallone. Culver City: Columbia Pictures, 2006.

[11] This phrase although not original to the Spider-Man series has been attributed to others in one form or another including Winston Churchill, Voltaire, and Roosevelt. I am referring here to the introduction of the phrase into U.S. pop culture in 1962.

[12] Norm Geisler. *Baker Encyclopedia of Christian Apologetics* (Grand Rapids: Baker Books, 1999.) 785.

[13] James Sire, *The Universe Next Door: A Basic Worldview Catalog, 4th Edition*, (Downers Grove: IVP Academic, 2004), 17.

[14] For a much more detailed discussion on this idea, I recommend you read through chapter 1 of Sire's work.

[15] Abdu Murray. *Grand Central Question: Answering the Critical Concerns of the Major Worldviews*. (Downers Grove: IVP, 2014), 31.

[16] Oxford Dictionaries, s.v. "religion" accessed May 11, 2016, http://www.oxforddictionaries.com/us/definition/american_english/religion

[17] Amy Orr-Ewing. "Postmodern Challenges to the Bible," in *Beyond Opinion*, Ed. Ravi Zacharias, (Nashville: Thomas Nelson, 2007), 3.

[18] These questions have been adopted and altered from James Sire, *The Universe Next Door*.

[19] Geisler. *Baker Encyclopedia of Christian Apologetics*, 786.

[20] R.C. Sproul. *Defending Your Faith: An Introduction to Apologetics*. (Wheaton: Crossway, 2003), 16.

[21] Taylor, *Introduction to Apologetics*, 19.

[22] Ibid., 19.

[23] C.S. Lewis, *On Obstinacy of Belief*, 186. Accessed via Creighton University. https://people.creighton.edu/~ees33175/God-Persons_website/GP_PDF-

readings/Lewis_Obstinacy-of-Faith.pdfhttps://people.creighton.edu/~ees33175/God-Persons_website/GP_PDF-readings/Lewis_Obstinacy-of-Faith.pdf

[24] Vern Sheridan Poythress. *Logic: A God-Centered Approach to the Foundation of Western Thought*, (Wheaton: Crossway, 2013), 126.

[25] J.P. Moreland and William Lane Craig. *Philosophical Foundations for a Christian Worldview*, (Downers Grove: IVP, 2003), 417.

[26] Poythress, *Logic*, 124.

CHAPTER 6

[27] Dictionary.com, s.v. "Faith," accessed February 2013, http://dictionary.reference.com/browse/faith?s=t.

[28] Miracle on 34th Street, directed by George Seaton, (New York: Twentieth Century Fox, 1947), DVD.

[29] H.L. Mencken. *Prejudices: Third Series*, (New York: Alfred A. Knopf, 1922), 267-68.

[30] William Lane Craig. *Reasonable Faith: Christian Truth and Apologetics, Third Edition*. (Wheaton: Crossway, 2008), 49-51.

[31] Geisler, *Baker Encyclopedia of Christian Apologetics*, 240.

[32] Thomas A. and Richard G. Howe, "Knowing Christianity is True: The Relationship Between Faith and Reason." *In Everyone an Answer*. Ed. Francis Beckwith, William Lane Craig and J.P. Moreland. (Downers Grove, InterVarsity Press: 2004), 36.

[33] Craig, *Reasonable Faith*, 51.

[34] Douglas Groothuis, *Christian Apologetics*, 119.

[35] Find this JP Moreland quote

[36] The Standford Encyclopedia of Philosophy, "The Coherence Theory of Truth" https://plato.stanford.edu/entries/truth-coherence/

[37] "Five Trends among the Unchurched," Barna Group, October 9, 2014, https://www.barna.org/barna-update/culture/685-five-trends-among-the-unchurched.

[38] Groothuis, *Christian Apologetics*, 128.

[39] Richard Dawkins. *The God Delusion* (Boston: Houghton Mifflin, 2006), 406.

[40] Stephen Hawking. *A Brief History of Time* (New York: Bantam, 1988), 122.

[41] John William Draper. *History of the Conflict Between Religion and Science* (New York: D. Appleton and Company, 1875), 363-364.

[42] Ibid., 363

[43] Ibid., 363

[44] Alister McGrath. *The Passionate Intellect: Christian Faith and the Discipleship of the Mind* (Downers Grove: InterVarsity Press, 2014), 110.

[45] Ibid., 110

[46] Ibid., 111

[47] Ibid., 111.

[48] http://www.merriam-webster.com/dictionary/science

[49] McGrath, *The Passionate Intellect*, 111.

[50] Nancy Pearcey. *Finding Truth: 5 Principles for Unmasking Atheism, Secularism, and Other God Substitutes* (Colorado Springs: David C. Cook, 2015), 197.

[51] Ibid., 197.

[52] Ibid., 196.

[53] Alister McGrath, *The Passionate Intellect*, 113.

[54] Ibid., 115.

[55] Michael Bird. *Evangelical Theology: A Biblical and Systematic Introduction* (Grand Rapids: Zondervan, 2013), 654.

[56] Ibid., 654.

[57] Ibid., 655.

[58] McGrath, *The Passionate Intellect*, 118.

[59] Ibid., 118.

[60] Friedrich Nietzsche, *The Gay Science* (New York: Barnes and Noble, Inc. 2008), 103.

CHAPTER 9

[61] *Bhagavad-Gita: The Song of God*, (New York: New American Library, 2002), 13.

[62] Sire, *The Universe Next Door*, p.145.

[63] Nietzsche, *The Gay Science*.

[64] These arguments are adapted from William Lane Craig, *Reasonable Faith: Christian Truth and Apologetics*. (Wheaton: Crossway, 2008).

CHAPTER 10

[65] This acronym is adapted *from Living Loud: Defending Your Faith*, Norman Geisler, and Joseph Holden. (Nashville: Broadman & Holman Publishers, 2002).

[66] This argument is partially adapted from Al-Ghazali's argument for God's existence. For a complete treatment of his argument see William Lane Craig's discussion on it in *On Guard*. p.74.

[67] William Lane Craig, *On Guard: Defending Your Faith With Reason And Precision*. (Colorado Springs: David C. Cook, 2010.), 77.

[68] Michael J. Behe, *Darwin's Black Box: The Biochemical Challenge to Evolution* (New York: The Free Press, 1996), 232.

[69] Sam Harris, *Moral Landscape: How Science Can Determine Human Values*, (New York: The Free Press, 2013), 6.

[70] Peter Singer, *The Expanding Circle: Ethics, Evolution, and Moral Progress*, (New Jersey: Princeton University Press, 1981), 27.

[71] This idea is taken from CS Lewis. *Christian Reflections*. (Grand Rapids, William B. Eerdmans, 1994.)

[72] Groothuis. *Christian Apologetics*, 343.

[73] Michael Bird. *Evangelical Theology*,

[74] Groothuis. *Christian Apologetics*, 94.

CHAPTER 11

[75] John Feinberg, *The Many Faces of Evil: Theological Systems and the Problems of Evil*. (Wheaton: Zondervan, 1994). Kindle location 258.

[76] Ibid., location 273.

[77] This line of argument summarizes the basic argumentation of the Greek Philosopher, Epicurus. who posed the question, "why would God allow evil to exist?" It essentially challenges the all-powerful and all-goodness of God and therefore challenges his ability to be God. John L. Mackie poised a more sophisticated form of Epicurus' argument. Mackie assumes that a perfectly good God always prevents evil, but since evil exists, God must not.

[78] Eleonore Stump, Norman Kretzmann, *The Cambridge Companion to Augustine*. (New York: Cambridge University Press, 2001), 40-48.

[79] Bird, *Evangelical Theology*, 687.

[80] Ibid., 687.

[81] Craig, *On Guard: Defending Your Faith with Reasons and Precision* (Colorado Springs: David C. Cook, 2010), 75.

[82] C.S. Lewis, *Mere Christianity* (1952; reprint, New Your: HarperCollins, 2001), 44.

[83] Bird, *Evangelical Theology*, 688.

[84] Alvin Plantinga, *God, Freedom, and Evil* (Grand Rapids: Wm B. Eerdmans, 1974). 29-34

[85] Ibid., 30.

[86] Ibid., 30.

[87] Garrett DeWeese, *God and Evil: The Case for God in a World Filled with Pain*, Edited by Chad Meister and James K. Dew, Jr. (Downers Grove: InterVarsity Press, 2012), 60-61.

[88] It is important here to note that when I am speaking of natural evils, I am speaking of the natural course of events in the world. This would, in my opinion, exclude supernatural events where God intervenes and even disrupts the natural. This would include God opening the earth and killing Korah's and his family, the parting of the Red Sea, Jesus calming the storm on the Sea of Galilee, and the many acts of healing throughout Scripture, etc.

CHAPTER 12

[89] William Lane Craig, "The Absurdity of Life without God," Reasonable Faith, accessed May 2015, http://www.reasonablefaith.org/the-absurdity-of-life-without-god.

CHAPTER 13

[90] Bertrand Russell, *Why I Am Not A Christian* (New York, Simon and Schuster, Inc., 1957), p. 16.

[91] See Baker Encyclopedia of Christian Apologetics, Dr. Norman Geisler.

[92] McDowell, *The New Evidence That Demands a Verdict*, (Nashville: Thomas Nelson, 1999), 34.

[93] Both charts are taken from The Bibliographical. Josh McDowell and Clay Jones. Updated August 13, 2014 (adapted from an earlier article by clay jones, the bibliographical test updated, Christian Research Journal, vol. 35, no. 3 (2012). Available at www.equip.org/articles/the-bibliographical-test-updated/)

[94] For details: www.biblequery.org

[95] Bruce M. Metzger and Bart D. Ehrman, *The Text of the New Testament: Its Transmission Corruption, and Restoration (4th Edition)* (Oxford: Oxford University Press, 2005), 34.

CHAPTER 14

[96] Charles Ryrie. Ryrie Study Bible: Expanded Edition, New International Version. (Chicago, Moody Press, 1984), 20.

[97] Ibid., 21.

CHAPTER 15

[98] Ibid., 84.

[99] Much of this information I attribute to Michael Bird, *Evangelical Theology: A Biblical and Systematic Introduction* (Grand Rapids: Zondervan, 2103), 470-472. Although he and other scholars include "S" as Jesus sits at the right hand of God on the throne. For the purposes of this text, I focused solely on the first four intending on simplicity.

[100] John R. W. Stott, *The Authentic Jesus* (London: Marshall, Morgan & Scott, 1985), 34.

[101] Bird, Evangelical Theology, 472.

[102] Wright, *The Challenge of Jesus: Rediscover Who Jesus Was and Is* (Downers Grove: IVP: 1999),121.

CHAPTER 16

[103] Gary Habermas, *The Historical Jesus: Ancient Evidence for the Life of Christ* (Joplin: College Press, 1996), 27.

[104] N.T. Wright, *Surprised By Hope: Rethinking Heaven, the Resurrection, and the Mission of the Church* (New York: HarperCollins, 2008 Kindle Edition), 67.

[105] Gary Habermas, *The Risen Jesus and Future Hope* (Lanham: Rowan & Littlefield, 2003), 163.

[106] Craig, William Lane (2014-04-03). Did Jesus Rise From the Dead? (Kindle Locations 223-225). Impact 360 Institute. Kindle Edition.

[107] John A. T. Robinson, *The Human Face of God* (Philadelphia: Westminster Press, 1973), 131.

[108] Josephus *Antiquities* 4.8.15

[109] Gary Habermas and Antony Flew, *Resurrected? An Atheist and Theist in Dialogue*, ed. John Ankerberg (Lanham: Rowman & Littlefield, 2005), 28.

[110] William Lane Craig Reasonable Faith, 361-377

[111] Gerd Ludeman, *The Resurrection of Christ: A Historical Inquiry* (New York: Prometheus Books, 2004), 37.

[112] Gary Habermas, "Tracing Jesus' Resurrection to Its Earliest Eyewitness Accounts," *God is Great, God is Good* (Downers Grove: InterVarsity Press, 2009), 212.

[113] N.T. Wright, *The Resurrection of the Son of God.* (Minneapolis: Fortress Press, 2003), 319.

[114] Craig, William Lane (2014-04-03). *Did Jesus Rise From the Dead?* (Kindle Locations 635-637). Impact 360 Institute. Kindle Edition.

[115] John Warwick Montgomery, *History, Law, and Christianity: A Vigorous, Convincing Presentation of the Evidence for a Historical Jesus* (Kindle Locations 993-994). (New Reformation Press. Kindle Edition).

[116] Ibid., (Kindle Locations 995-999).

[117] Tacitus, *Annals* 15.44

[118] Habermas, *The Historical Jesus,* 191.

[119] Suetonius, *Claudius,* 25.

[120] Josephus, *Antiquities,* 20.200

[121] C.S. Lewis. Mere Christianity

[122] Michael Bird, *Evangelical Theology,* 440-41.

[123] Craig, *Did Jesus Rise From the Dead?* (Kindle Locations 829-832).

[124] Wright, *Surprised By Hope.* 67.

Made in the USA
Lexington, KY
31 January 2018